AF087766

Goddess *Within* Oracle

Healing with
the Divine Feminine

Christabel Jessica

....

Art by Cecilia G.F.
& Dannielle Jones

GODDESS WITHIN ORACLE
Healing with the Divine Feminine

Copyright © 2024 Christabel Jessica
Artwork by Cecilia G.F. listed on page 144
Artwork by Dannielle Jones listed on page 145

All rights reserved. Other than for personal use, no part of these cards or this book may be reproduced in any way, in whole or part, without the written consent of the copyright holder or publisher. These cards are intended for spiritual and emotional guidance only. They are not intended to replace medical assistance or treatment.

Published by Blue Angel Publishing®
80 Glen Tower Drive, Glen Waverley,
Victoria, Australia 3150
E-mail: info@blueangelonline.com
Website: www.blueangelonline.com

Edited by Marie DelBalso and Peter Loupelis

Blue Angel is a registered trademark of
Blue Angel Gallery, Pty. Ltd.

ISBN: 978-1-922573-79-7

Dedicated to returning
power to the feminine,
unlocking her wild heart,
and acknowledging and
releasing her pain to allow
her to run free.

CONTENTS

The Rise of the Divine Feminine   7
The Purpose of This Oracle   10
Mythology   11
Working with This Oracle   12
How to Use the Cards   13
The Divine Feminine Card Spreads   18

CARD MEANINGS
Anahit   24
Aphrodite   26
Artemis   28
Athena   30
Baba Yaga   32
Baubo   34
Boudicca   37
Brigid   39
Cerridwen   42
Cleopatra   45
Demeter   47
Durga   50
Estsanatlehi   53
Eve   55
Freyja   58
Hecate   61
Hina   63
Inanna   65
Isis   68

Ixcacao   71
Ixchel   74
Joan of Arc   76
Kali Ma   78
Lady of the Lake   81
Lilith   84
Ma'at   87
Mary Magdalene   90
Medusa   93
Musso Koroni   96
Nyx   99
Oya   102
Pachamama   105
Pandora   108
Persephone   110
Quan Yin   113
Queen Maya   116
Queen of Sheba   119
Sedna   122
Sekhmet   125
Sheela Na Gig   128
The Morrighan   131
Thetis   133
Walu   136
White Buffalo Calf Woman   139

About the Author   143
About the Artists   144
Blue Angel Publishing   147

THE RISE OF THE DIVINE FEMININE

Once upon a time, in a magical land, a maiden stood barefoot in the grass at midnight, basking in the soft glow of the full moon. Invoking her goddesses and ancestors, she stepped into the river, connected with the elements and released all that no longer served her.

During the same full moon, an introverted crone stood in her cottage in the woods on the other side of the village. An owl screeched overhead as she prepared herbal blends for the villagers to assist them with their pregnancies and illnesses.

Across the sea, a priestess lit a candle in her temple, preparing to work in ceremony for the soldiers passing through on their way back from war-ravaged lands. Sharing her healing energy and sexuality, the priestess eased the horrors and trauma of wartime.

Spread throughout the lands, under the brightly lit moon, many more women connected to Mother Gaia's graces and channelled the energies of the Divine as an anchor of light. These women stood tall in their many roles as healers — the priestess, oracle, pagan, mystic, herbalist and medicine woman.

The morning after the full moon, after murmurs

of a maiden's ceremony, a group of townspeople bound the young woman, accusing her of being a witch. A week later, she was burned at the stake as her mother and sister watched. Her sister, also a pagan, never worked in ceremony again.

The crone concocting healing blends in her cottage once lived in the nearby village. When she was a young woman, she was due to marry a man who loved her deeply until whispers that her healing ability was linked to forbidden worship circulated. She never married, and only those brave and desperate sought her counsel. She lived alone, with the land supporting her, until the day she died.

The priestess in her temple was called scarlet and dragged through the streets by her beautiful, long red hair. She never recovered and felt fear each time she attempted to channel her healing energy. She vowed to remain celibate for life, with the power of this vow echoing into her future lifetimes.

Stories like these are common. After all, women have been scapegoated since the dawn of religion. There are origin stories of women causing the first sin by eating forbidden fruit or unleashing all evil by opening a box. How are women to be trusted? Though the masculine has also been repressed, that is a story for another day.

Those not standing in their power feared the

potency of the in-tune woman and did everything they could to repress this innate power and strip the healing arts from Earth. Yes, that magical land was Earth. And now, the Divine Feminine is rising. After an age ruled by patriarchy, the feminine is taking her rightful place beside the masculine.

It is becoming safer for women to come forward as powerful beings. The time of threat is slowly yet surely drawing to a close, and the re-emergence of creatrix energy is happening. Women are stepping more and more into their power as each day passes. It was not long ago that women were not allowed to vote, have credit cards, attend university or build a career. With the breaking down of the patriarchal framework via the granting of rights and the space to safely display power comes a time to work through the collective pain, the persecution energy and fears of speaking up and being seen. Hence this deck. It is time to release the trauma, repressed emotions, fears and antiquated templates built into a repressive society. It is time to harness the Divine Feminine's energy readily available to you.

As Earth steps out of the Age of Pisces and into the Age of Aquarius, old paradigms are shedding, making way for a rebirth. Welcome to the dawn of a new cycle, and thank you for being a part of the expansion of consciousness.

THE PURPOSE OF THIS ORACLE

These cards were created in honour of women in all phases — inner child, maiden, mother, crone and all aspects between. This deck is for *anyone* who wants to explore and connect with their divine feminine energy — not just women but also those who identify as male or non-binary. Working with feminine energy is like a warm hug from a loving mother — everyone deserves this. Each person has masculine and feminine energies in varying degrees, so we can all benefit from receiving the healing available to us through working with both. Working with each energy polarity within you balances yin and yang and leads to becoming an integrated, whole being. And the place where masculine and feminine meet in the middle provides healing through balance and non-binary energy.

Take a walk through history, connecting with heroines, queens and goddesses of various pantheons, ages and energies. Some will call on you to feel deeply. Others will call on you to learn something new or to activate an aspect of your essence. Allow each card to take you on a journey deep within as they bring forward the teaching and healing frequency relevant to you. Over time, you will integrate these energies. Each embodiment of the Divine Feminine within this deck will surround you with love, support and guidance, ensuring you are not alone on the path of humanity.

MYTHOLOGY

Mythology provides insight into how society has conducted itself in the past and how society views itself today. Mythology is not about whether the events took place but what the stories represent. Passed down through generations, they reveal societal values and perspectives. The language, themes and aspects of the stories that are frowned upon or celebrated can give you direct insight into how humans view themselves, then and now. This gives you access to limiting beliefs you may unknowingly hold so you may question them. Your psyche may contain 'egregores'—group thought forms—that are a direct result of repetitive exposure to mythological stories. Perhaps there are things you judge yourself on based on inherited beliefs passed down that weasel their way in via your self-talk narrative. Questioning the narrative of how society was formed and the influencing events is a great way to dive into transformative work.

WORKING WITH THIS ORACLE

Refer to your cards when you want the loving support and guided lessons of the Divine Feminine. This deck is filled with feminine energy. Use it when you are experiencing heavy emotions or need clarity and be embraced in her knowing hug. The Divine Feminine is fierce, soft, bold, nurturing, gentle, unrelenting and always loving. When overwhelmed, she will soothe and rock you to sleep, and when you need to implement change, she will be the stern mother telling you the uncomfortable truth. She will give you the medicine you need—even when it is bitter—for she knows you deserve to feel better.

    Work with these cards when you need direction for deciding how to handle your current circumstances. Your fate is never set in stone. This deck does not predict the future but offers insight, clarity and encouragement to use your free will to determine your destiny. The Divine Feminine recognises your power to create the life you desire.

HOW TO USE THE CARDS

The following instructions are suggestions to help you get started. There are no rules. Instead of feeling dictated to or restricted to working with your deck in a certain way, approach your cards however it feels good for you. Have fun, play, experiment and enjoy freedom within your oracle experience.

When first handling your oracle deck, take some time to develop a personal connection with your cards. You may like to create a sacred space where you can be present with the cards in ritual. A ritual can be as simple as walking barefoot in the grass or sitting in a favourite chair as you connect with your deck. For something more elaborate, add ceremonial elements, such as lighting a dedicated candle, burning essential oils or placing your favourite crystal near the deck. When your space is ready, energetically clear your deck (see *Clearing Your Cards*, over page).

With your space and cards prepared, sit in quiet meditation with one hand underneath and one over the deck. Using your breath to centre yourself, focus your attention on how the deck feels. Invoke the Divine Feminine to infuse your cards with healing energy. Sit in meditation for as long as you feel comfortable.

Next, complete a card reading in honour of the deck itself. Ask for a card to represent the relationship you will share energetically, a second card to represent you and a third card to represent the deck. This will help facilitate deeper connections between yourself, the messages, the imagery and the Divine Feminine.

Another way to connect with your deck is to place it next to your pillow for seven nights as you sleep. Naturally, your relationship with your cards will continue to deepen as you work with them.

Clearing Your Cards

Regularly refresh your cards, so they are always at the highest vibration for accurate readings. Tap the deck three times as a quick and easy way to clear away residual energies before a reading.

Other ways of clearing your deck include smoke cleansing, sound bowl cleansing or placing the deck by a window in the light of the full moon. Between readings, you may like to set your deck in a bowl of salt or sit a crystal with a cleansing frequency on top of the deck. I like to use selenite, clear quartz or black tourmaline.

How to Do a Reading

Close your eyes and centre yourself. Anchor your energy to Mother Gaia by placing your feet flat on the floor and feeling your physical connection to the earth. Place one hand over your heart and the other over the cards. In your mind or out loud, call on your guides and your higher self to be present with you. You can use an invocation, such as:

My highest level guides from the highest realms, please be with me and help me gain insight through these cards.

Bring your focus to the situation you are seeking guidance on. Hold your cards and formulate a question. The more detailed your question, the more focused the reading's intention becomes. Begin shuffling the cards in any way that feels comfortable to you. If you are new to pulling cards, be patient as you learn to intuit how long to shuffle and which cards to draw. There is no right or wrong. With practice, you will start to feel more sure of yourself.

Cards that fall from the deck as you shuffle are strong messages asking for your attention. Include them in your reading, and trust that it leapt out for a reason.

When you need clarity about a card in a layout, draw another card to give more information. This clarifier card builds upon the cards already chosen and deepens the message.

Interpreting the Message

Each card is infused with an energetic transmission of the Divine Feminine. The card descriptions are written in a way that guides you to understand and adapt to the energies impacting you. Each card represents an aspect of being human and the healing path.

When you read the card messages, take note of the words that resonate with you. Take them on and expand your perspective for insight into your question. A card's meaning can vary each time it appears in a reading. You could pull the same card every day for a week and interpret it differently depending on what is surfacing for you on that day.

Understanding the meaning of your chosen cards may come instantly or after some reflection and contemplation. Look at the card's image and notice what comes to mind. The card name, symbolism, colours, body language or facial expressions may bring you a feeling or thought.

Sit with the imagery of each card, allowing your mind time to process it. When you are ready, read the card meanings and feel the guidance as it pertains to your question. To gain inspiration on how to tackle your situation, read the story of the Divine Feminine that represents the card.

You do not need to come to one meaning. You are a multifaceted being — allow each part of you to have a voice. Your inner child will speak a different thought to you than your higher self, as will your intuition and logic. The point is not to know which part of you expresses each thought or feeling. Instead, allow space for the vastness of all you are. Your subconscious and conscious minds will work together to bring you meaning from your guides, as will your intuition and logic. Take your time and write down any information that comes through to you. Some thoughts and feelings are fleeting, and sitting with them will be enough to allow for processing. Other themes will require more time to play out. You may like to explore your reading through journalling. Over time, reading your journal entries can give you deeper insight into how you feel about a situation and how you would like to move forward.

THE DIVINE FEMININE CARD SPREADS

Single-card Spread
A one-card spread gets to the heart of a situation. Larger spreads have their time and place, but for a straightforward answer or when you don't feel the need to dive into the layers of your situation, go for a one-card spread. Use this spread to tune in to the overall energy of the query or to answer a specific question. You can use a one-card spread to represent the energy of the day, week or month.

Two-card Spread
Two-card spreads are valuable in situations with a dualistic nature and provide clarity in simple decision-making. Be clear about the two sides you are weighing up. Assign one side Card One and the other Card Two. Shuffle the deck, select your cards and lay them down side by side. Interpret each card to give you insight into each option's benefits, challenges and lessons.

Some examples of dualistic meanings you can assign for a two-card spread include:

Do/don't
Query/solution
Yes/no
Past/present
Mind/heart
Logic/emotions
Comfort/lesson
Feel/do

Three-card Spread

More elaborate than the energies of a one or two-card spread, a three-card spread provides you with deeper insight into the layers of your query. Pulling three cards—to represent the past (Card One), present (Card Two) and future (Card Three)—provides a glimpse into where you've been, where you are now, and where you are headed.

Another option for a three-card spread includes using Card One to represent the energy of a situation, Card Two to represent the most significant obstacle at hand and Card Three to determine how to overcome the obstacle.

Four-card Spread

Use a four-card spread to conduct a deep soul search and to reach the core of multiple aspects of a situation.

The Yoni Layout

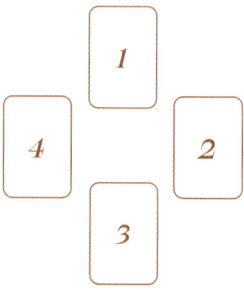

This spread offers insight by exploring four aspects of the situation at hand: light (embrace), shadow (face), inner (internal energy) and outer (external energy).

Card 1: What do I need to embrace about this situation?
Card 2: What do I need to face about this situation?
Card 3: How is my inner being affecting this situation?
Card 4: How are my outer circumstances affecting this situation?

The Nourish Layout

This spread shows you the energy your inner child, mind, body and soul currently require for nourishment.

Card 1: What does my inner child require to feel nourished?
Card 2: What does my mind need to be at its most nourished state?
Card 3: What does my body need to feel nourished?
Card 4: What does my soul need to be nourished?

The Energetic Scan Layout

Another option for a four-card spread is to pull a card to represent the root of the situation's emotional, mental, physical and spiritual energy.

Card 1: Which card represents my emotional energy?
Card 2: Which card represents my mental energy?
Card 3: Which card represents my physical energy?
Card 4: Which card represents my spiritual energy?

CARD MEANINGS

ANAHIT

Work on your relationship with your body by honouring it as the vessel through which you experience life.

In Armenian mythology, Anahit is the goddess of fertility, healing, wisdom and water. Introduced during the fifth century BCE, she became one of several primary deities worshipped in Armenia, alongside Aramazd. Described as the mother of Armenian paganism, statues of the goddess emerged throughout Armenia during the rise of her popularity, signifying her importance. Today, the bronze head of the deity can be viewed at the British Museum. With her connection to water, the source of life and her healing powers, people with any illnesses or physical ailments would travel to the temples in Artashat to worship her and receive help and healing.

Anahit's Message
Your body is incredible and deserves your unconditional love and respect. It is the reason you are able to taste, touch and experience life. Do you catch yourself

thinking you will wait until your imperfections improve before booking that beach vacation or going out for a night of dancing? When looking at yourself in the mirror, do you tend to hone in on the areas you have deemed not good enough?

When another person looks at you, they see the whole of you. They are zoomed out, whereas you are zoomed in. Others see how your face lights up when you smile; they see how you shine like the sun when you share a joke. They do not hone in on imperfections as you do.

The human body is the vessel through which your soul gets to experience this world, allowing you access to pleasure and joy. Through your body, you can taste chocolate cake, smell the beautiful perfume of flowers, and revel in the joy of laughter and the feel of silky, beautiful fabrics draped over you. Your body anchors you to the earth as you press your hands into the soil of your garden, feel the grass under your feet and the sunshine penetrating your skin.

From this moment, there is no more waiting until your flaws are 'fixed' before allowing yourself to enjoy your body. Your life is happening now. Make a practice of looking in the mirror zoomed out. List how your body will enable you to experience its beauty and notice your relationship with your body shift.

APHRODITE

Use your heartbreak to heal, dive into your heart, feel your pain and emerge with an openness to love.

In the Greek pantheon, Aphrodite is heralded as the goddess of love, passion, lust, sexuality and beauty. Aphrodite emerged from the white foam stirred up in the sea by the severed genitalia of the sky god Ouranos. Born from the ocean, she is worshipped as a sea and seafaring goddess. Aphrodite is associated with the element of water—representing emotions—and with Venus, the planet of love and beauty. Although many tales are told about Aphrodite, none are more sought out than her love affairs. Some of her lovers include Ares, the god of war; Adonis, the god of beauty and desire; and Anchises, a mortal Trojan prince.

Aphrodite's Message

Your ability to love brings your life meaning and joy but can also be a source of immense pain. During times of heartbreak, you may feel that the grief will split you in two, and you may vow never to put yourself in that position again. It is understandable to want to shield your heart and protect it. If you never loved, you would never feel heartbreak, yet you would never truly live.

Allow yourself a period of retreat to process your feelings of grief, betrayal and disappointment. Seek space to turn inward as you hold yourself through grieving the loss of the future you imagined. Reach out to your loved ones when needed, communicate how they can help you feel connection and love as you adjust to your loss: hugs, quality time or talking.

Heartbreak serves a purpose — it is a cleanser, a healer, a teacher and a fortifier. A heart in pain breaks open, allowing you to mend what is within. It rips you wide open and brings to the surface emotional pain connected not only to this situation but also to childhood, past relationships and even past lives. Feeling the pain deeply allows cleansing and healing; a heart that can be re-knit and fortified in strength becomes resilient. Heartbreak teaches you how to love and discern where to place your love.

When moving forward, you have two choices: be brave and keep your heart as a flower in bloom, or close it down and become hardened. The bravery is well worth it; love after heartbreak runs stronger than ever before.

ARTEMIS

Embrace the energy of new beginnings, passion and action by honouring your inner Maiden.

ARTEMIS

One of the twelve Olympians who ruled the universe from atop Mount Olympus, Artemis is the Greek goddess of the hunt. Daughter to Zeus and twin sister to Apollo, she is associated with wild animals, the wilderness, the moon, chastity and virginity. As a small child, Artemis asked her father for a bow and quiver of arrows. Zeus ordered the three Cyclopes to craft these for her from silver. Thus she was never seen without them again. Artemis never used her weapon to hurt but instead used it to protect wild animals. Not a fan of men, she never married and vowed to remain a virgin. Instead, she dreamed of roaming the wilderness for all her days.

Artemis' Message

By honouring the Maiden, you can emulate and embody her energy to draw upon as you walk forward on your path. To do so is to celebrate the goddess as her first archetype. This aspect of the goddess tells the story of entering adulthood and promising exciting new beginnings and adventures. She models and radiates passion and the illumination of the soul through grand expansion. Her enthusiasm is like a breath of fresh air and fills her with the energy required to venture out on a soul quest.

The Maiden is the one who stands at the beginning of the yellow brick road, ready to journey forward, seeking the wisdom of the wizard. Not yet knowing, the journey will teach her to access the seed of knowledge ready to hatch within. It was already there as she took her first step onto the path. With each new step on her journey forward, she discovers the blooming of this seed through her experiences as they become the fertiliser for growth.

The Maiden musters her courage as she ventures forth through the woods learning whom to trust, how to read people and how to discern truth from lies, love from lust and wise choices from poor choices.

Each mistake the Maiden makes, each shocking betrayal bestowed upon her, takes her on a more profound journey within her soul. Yet, as she stumbles, she stands back up with insurmountable energy and a passion bursting forth as she springs back into action, following the path in front of her. Activate the Maiden that lives within you as you venture forth on your path of seeking and learning.

ATHENA

Listen to your fear as it guides you towards removing something from your life or encourages you to jump out of your comfort zone towards exciting new opportunities.

Athena is the Olympian goddess of wisdom and war, known as Athens' patron deity. Uninterested in romantic relationships, Athena remained a virgin. Known for her influential contributions to battle, she used her mind, wit and wisdom to strategise expertly. She is said to be Zeus' favourite daughter for assisting him in winning a fight against the giants. Consulted by many gods and goddesses, Athena played a vital role in many Greek legends. Heracles, feeling particularly grateful for her assistance, gifted Athena the apples of the Hesperides. To thank her for helping him slay Medusa, Perseus gave the Gorgon's head to Athena, which she hung from her shield.

Athena's Message

Fear is a natural part of the human experience and can be used to your advantage. It is not the enemy. Instead, it is an alert system your nervous system uses to keep you safe. This stems from the beginning of humankind, when fear alerted humans to imminent danger from physical threats, such as predators. Your brain signals your body, letting you know it is time for either fight or flight. Your heart rate quickens, your breath changes, and the stress hormones adrenaline and cortisol are released into your bloodstream. Alternatively, you may experience a freeze response which brings a decreased heartbeat, a feeling of an inability to move and restricted breath.

When you feel fear arising, ask yourself what it is alerting you to. It can be one of two things — asking you to turn away from danger or signalling you to jump out of your comfort zone. If your answer is to turn away, do what you need to make yourself safe. It is okay to be scared when you are directed towards conquering something out of your comfort zone. Be gentle with yourself throughout this process.

Conquering fear requires you to focus on how much you truly desire what is on the other side. Rather than waiting for the fear to pass, the key is to face it even though you are scared. Fear dissipates through action, not by waiting for the fear to pass before acting. Being afraid and doing it anyway allows for growth. There is no bravery without fear.

BABA YAGA

Bring forth your fierce, bold nature from deep within. This life is temporary, so be wild and take a chance on yourself rather than playing it safe.

Translating to 'wicked grandmother', Baba Yaga is a feared figure in Russian mythology. Tales of her folklore have been a source of penetrating fear for centuries, particularly stories involving her eating children. A witch living in a hut built with chicken legs, Baba Yaga is a trickster who either helps or hinders those who cross her path. She is the embodiment of the wild woman living on the outskirts of society, not caring what anyone thinks and conforming to no rules. Viewed as a goddess of regeneration, Baba Yaga is known as the 'old woman of autumn.' She is associated with the last harvested grain, with an old wives' tale that if a woman were to consume this grain, they would fall pregnant.

Baba Yaga's Message
Now is not the time to play it safe or make yourself small and quiet to appease another. Be bold, assertive and

unapologetic. Instead of appeasing the people around you, let them hear every step you take. You may find this difficult because humans are biologically driven to fit in with their clans to survive. You are encouraged to mentally override this schema and march to the beat of your drum.

Do you make decisions that go along with convention to feel safe? In a world that can seem brutal, unaccepting and backwards, perhaps it's not such a bad thing to be seen as different. It is time to get comfortable with the qualities of being a revolutionary. Do you imagine what the world would be like with radical paradigm shifts and hope to be a facilitator of this? Look at the way the revolutionaries you admire were treated and seen by their peers in their time. They all had similar stories; they were often seen as weird, mocked and sometimes imprisoned or killed.

Innovation requires being bold and ahead of the curve. It requires being comfortable with not fitting in and, most importantly, not being tamed. Question the way things are done in the world at large and in your life. What patterns do you maintain that don't match your wildness? It is time to unleash your inner badass and be bold, rejecting the traditional mould. Life is fulfilling when you release the shackles of society's boxes and release your fear of going against the grain.

BAUBO

Find levity in the madness of Earth and view human nature through the eyes of humour. Laughter can bring joy to the darkest of moments.

Baubo is an ancient Greek goddess mainly spoken of in myths from the early Orphic religion. As the goddess of mirth, she is celebrated for her liberated nature. A fun-loving older woman, Baubo exhibits her wisdom through laughter and jesting. Humorously dealing with sexuality, Baubo is the epitome of the untamed woman. She is a central figure in the story of Demeter and her daughter Persephone. After Hades—the god of the underworld—abducted Persephone, Baubo was the first to make Demeter laugh through her grief. Offering her a drink, Demeter refused. So, Baubo lifted her dress to show her private parts, ultimately making Demeter laugh.

Baubo's Message

When life throws you curve balls, finding moments of joy in the chaos can be challenging. Seeking pleasure is essential because you are only on this beautiful planet temporarily. Think about the things an angel would want to experience as a human — delicious food, dancing to music, beautiful beaches, physical intimacy and deep belly laughs. Intentionally create opportunities for joy, laughter and the lighter side of life.

Human existence can feel incredibly dense for highly sensitive people. It can feel like drudging through a pool full of mud. But that's not all you are intended to experience. You are here for both sides of the equation. You are here for duality — the contrast found at either end of the spectrum. You need joy to complement the hard work of mortal existence.

The balancing of these polarities applies to spiritual work as well. Cleansing old, energetic debris through your work in the emotional realm is intended to make way for new energy to fill you back up. Releasing without refilling will leave you depleted. So ensure you replenish yourself with light after the hard work of clearing difficult emotions.

There is a reason why the saying "laughter is the best medicine" is often quoted — it's because the essence of laughter can heal at a level so deep it can reach you at your core. A sense of humour is a gift of alchemy bestowed upon humanity. It is how humans can transmute in the most magnificent, joyous way! It is a way to reclaim your power from the clutches of despair.

Seeing life's pitfalls through a lens of humour can be the remedy to density. Lift the burden from your shoulders — laugh!

BOUDICCA

Instead of waiting for motivation to move you, move towards your goals and feel the flow of inspiration.

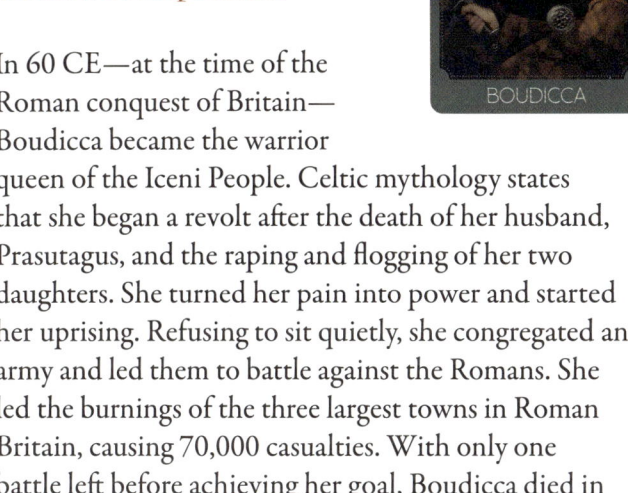

In 60 CE—at the time of the Roman conquest of Britain—Boudicca became the warrior queen of the Iceni People. Celtic mythology states that she began a revolt after the death of her husband, Prasutagus, and the raping and flogging of her two daughters. She turned her pain into power and started her uprising. Refusing to sit quietly, she congregated an army and led them to battle against the Romans. She led the burnings of the three largest towns in Roman Britain, causing 70,000 casualties. With only one battle left before achieving her goal, Boudicca died in 61 CE. She represents bravery and taking action amid oppression.

Boudicca's Message
The time for sitting back and being passive is over. You are ready to take inspired action. Intuitive people on a spiritual path can find it difficult to leave the

meditative bubble and put their intuition into action. Daydreaming about the future you desire is essential in the manifestation process, but more is required.

Without implemented action, a goal is merely a dream. To bring a vision into reality, you must decide on an action step that can start bringing about that desire. Striking a balance between mind and heart is paramount. In a world of duality, people tend to swing towards the extremes without even realising it.

Taking unplanned action or a blind reaction to an emotional charge can lead you to a path without direction or fulfilment. On the other hand, receiving intuitive guidance, ignoring that information and taking no action leads to stagnation. It can be a pitfall on a spiritual path to wait for the Universe to interject or to wait for fate or destiny to bring things in with no steps taken to allow for the fruition of goals.

It is easy to fall into the trap of waiting for the right time, for things to feel guaranteed or for all the steps to make sense so that the whole picture is illuminated. Instead of waiting for the right moment, taking action will open up your timelines and allow the next opportunity or idea to present itself. So take charge of your destiny and go for it!

BRIGID

Cultivate your abilities to hone in on intuitive messages and inspirations that come through as seeds of ideas.

BRIGID

Brigid—also referred to as the Exalted One—is a Celtic goddess associated with fire, spring, inspiration, divination, fertility and smithcraft. A patron of healing and the arts, Brigid is a guiding goddess for those who conduct poetry, prophecy and other forms of healing wisdom. She is the personification of the fires of inspiration. Brigid is one of the principal deities of pre-Christian Gaelic Ireland, otherwise known as the Tuatha Dé Danann. Married to Bres, the ruler of the Tuatha Dé Danann, Brigid was a patron of warfare with a band of soldiers under her called 'brigands'. According to another version of her mythology, Brigid is believed to be Saint Brigid of Kildare, born in Ireland in the 1300s.

Brigid's Message

Learn to harness the sparks of intuition that ask to be heard, turning them into flames of inspiration and creativity. The more you understand how you receive guidance, the more you can actively use your intuition rather than it happening passively without you noticing.

Your intuition whispers, whereas the mind speaks louder. Becoming aware of these messages takes practice. When you become attuned to these whispers, you can grab hold of the ideas being brought to you. Building your understanding of psychic abilities can help create your reference points.

Think of these messages as guidance that emerges via your psychic abilities. Some will see; others will hear, feel or know. Once you recognise the inspiration, it is time to use it. It can be difficult to take the seed of inspiration, step into spiritual action and turn it into something tangible.

You will be given a little nugget of inspiration, and it may be challenging to get motivated to take that nugget and bring it into form. The secret is to start the action for the motivation to come. When you have the nugget of an idea, you have all you need to start — so take the first step!

The flow from the first step of putting that idea into motion creates incentive. The things that are unhealthiest for you feel good *before* you do them, and the things that are healthy for you feel good *after*. For example, binge eating and watching television gives you dopamine before, while going for a workout provides you dopamine after the activity.

Rather than waiting for motivation, take that first step and let it kick in afterwards. Listen to your intuitive messages to inspire you to put them into action and to motivate you to follow the lead and be inspired to take more intuitive guidance.

CERRIDWEN

Respect the Crone and bring introspection to her archetype within you. She is an embodiment of wisdom for serving yourself and those around you.

In Welsh lore, Cerridwen is a crone known as an enchantress, hag, shapeshifter and goddess of the underworld. She is the keeper of the cauldron of knowledge, which some believe to be the Holy Grail. Her name is a derivative of *cerru*, the Celtic word for 'cauldron' and is associated with transformation, poetry and prophecy. Mother to daughter Creirwy and ugly son Morfran, Cerridwen brewed a potion to transform her son. Her servant Gwion accidentally consumed the potion. He shapeshifted into a hare to escape his mistress, resulting in a chase through the seasons with both Cerridwen and Gwion disguised in different forms. The chase ended when Cerridwen took the form of a hen and swallowed Gwion, who was hiding as a grain of corn.

Cerridwen's Message

To celebrate the Crone is to honour the final aspect of the goddess, the third representation of the circle of life. She understands that the more you learn, the less you know and that becoming a master means becoming the fool again. She knows the Maiden and the Mother voyages have been vital aspects to the journey of the wise woman, for both carried incomplete and unrefined versions of the future Crone within them.

As the Crone journeyed through the paths of maidenhood and motherhood, the tiny seed within grew through the life experiences laid before her. It's not that the seed wasn't there initially, but life experience gave it space to sprout to fruition, allowing it to become a beautiful oak tree. Each branch represents a fork in the road of her many former selves. Each leaf represents a decision, a mistake, a hurt, a love or a heartbreak that blossomed into wisdom garnered through experience. This wisdom brings forth the ability to look back in hindsight at why certain things had to happen and why particular doors had to close.

The Crone can be a frightening figure to those who do not yet understand her and her untamed nature. She who deserves the most reverence can incite the most substantial feelings of confrontation in those still enamoured with the ideas of beauty associated with youth. The Crone's beauty holds a depth that youth cannot match and should be respected for holding. The wisdom from a long life lived is a privilege and a beauty to behold with its richness and depth.

Honour the Crone; she will guide you forward with her wisdom, compassion and knowledge.

CLEOPATRA

Karmic influences affect your current circumstances, and energetic patterns are ready to be transformed.

Heralded as one of ancient Egypt's most eminent rulers, Cleopatra, born in 69 BCE, has been a source of divine feminine power to be drawn upon since her reign. Although born in Egypt, she was the last ruler of the Ptolemaic dynasty, making her a descendant of a Macedonian Greek general. Not afraid to stand in power bestowed upon her, Cleopatra claimed to be the goddess Isis incarnate. She is remembered for her intellect, strength and love relationships with Julius Caesar and Mark Antony. To this day, academia debates the cause of her death. A widely accepted theory is that Cleopatra enticed an asp to bite her to end her life. At the same time, Mark Antony stabbed himself in the stomach after losing a battle against the Roman leader Octavian.

Cleopatra's Message
A lifetime is a mere blink of an eye for the soul. However, you are made up of much more than what

your pragmatic memory allows you to see about yourself. You hold within your blueprint the karmic residue of your entire soul history and that of your ancestral line. These energies present themselves in all areas of your life and are here to serve as your lessons and fodder for growth and change.

Have you ever had an experience that evoked such a strong emotional response that left you confused about why it felt so intense? This situation had karmic influences that struck a chord deep within your soul. The memories in your Akashic records emerge as these responses to patterns that repeat themselves in your life.

Karmic lessons can be identified by examining the situations, relationships and behaviours that seem to show up in your life continuously. Unresolved karmic energy grows in magnitude and frequency to shove the core issues right in your face. These lessons help you shift these old karmic influences and overcome them by breaking the energetic cycle.

Each time the situation cycles, look back to see how far you have come. Instead of thinking, "Why me?" think, "What can I learn from this?" When you take a situation that you perceive to be negative and figure out a way to learn from it or shift it into a new way of reacting, then you have harnessed the power of karma to be a catalyst for change.

DEMETER

Instead of forcing the situations in your life to come to fruition prematurely, allow them to unfold and mature with a strong foundation.

In ancient Greek mythology, Demeter—one of the twelve Olympians—is the goddess of the harvest, corn and agriculture. Daughter of the Titans Cronus and Rhea, she is associated with sacred law and the cycle of life and death. When her daughter, Persephone, was abducted by Hades, Demeter was so inconsolable that she wandered the lands of Greece searching for her. During the winter and autumn months, the earth became barren as she mourned the loss of her daughter. With Persephone's return in spring, Demeter's grief lifted, and with that, the lands became nourished and rife with harvest once more. The myth of Demeter is used to explain the seasonal cycle and the importance of a fruitful harvest.

Demeter's Message

Imagine buying some rose seedlings. You come home and plant them in the garden. Barely able to wait for these seeds to become beautiful flowers, you are beyond excited. Deciding you cannot wait, you immediately water and tend to them frequently throughout the day in your desire to make them grow. Without the time to go through the growing phase, these seeds now become waterlogged and die before having the chance to bloom. Humans tend to do this with new relationships, creative projects and opportunities.

With the excitement to attain the finished product, the human tendency is to crush the rose before it's had time to unfurl its beautiful petals. Forcing an idea to fruition can kill it before it's had a chance to grow.

To allow natural unfolding is to hold space for the energies and the processes to come to fruition in time. A lack of patience can signify an unconscious belief that the unfolding will not happen, so you must rush it and cling tight to ensure it works out.

Suppose you have an internalised insecurity that you are not lovable and that everyone abandons you. In that case, you may try to rush a newfound romantic interest into a commitment phase instead of enjoying the flirty dating stage. Suppose you have an internal belief system correlated with an inability to succeed. In that case, you may rush the steps of your career instead of enjoying the building of a strong foundation and creation phase.

    Your desire to push things forwards indicates that it is time to ground yourself in the present moment and assess why you have the urge to rush. You deserve to enjoy the unfolding of your life. Be patient, and trust that it will happen as it needs to.

DURGA

Contemplate your boundaries, communicate them clearly and dedicate yourself to enforcing them vigorously.

Revered as a Hindu deity, Durga is worshipped as the protective mother of the universe. In Sanskrit, her name translates to 'fort', or a protected place. In Hindu mythology, Durga was created by the gods to destroy a mighty demon that only a female could overcome. She has been watching over the universe and protecting it from evil ever since. Durga possesses multiple arms so she can defend herself from every direction. She embodies feminine strength and is often depicted atop a tiger, riding into battle. Her symbolism includes the conch shell to represent the power of sound, the lotus flower to represent detachment and the colour red to symbolise action.

Durga's Message

Your boundaries determine what you allow into your personal space, life and energy field. Boundaries are your limits and clear guidelines that are already a part of so many areas of your life without you thinking about it! They protect you in the following areas: material, physical, mental, emotional, energetic, love, spiritual and more. For example, locking your doors at night creates a boundary so that you are safe and people don't walk into your house and help themselves to the food in your fridge. However, in other areas of your life, your boundaries may not be as apparent to you and the people around you. Bring awareness to what constitutes a boundary for you, and you will prevent your energy from leaking or being robbed by others.

    Once you are clear on your boundaries, communicate them with the people around you and let them know the consequence of not respecting them. The most vital thing to understand is that it isn't the job of others to obey them, but your responsibility to enforce them.

    When your boundaries have been violated, it is up to you to facilitate the consequences. For example, you have a boundary around preventing close friends or family from interfering in your love life more than is acceptable to you. If you are speaking on the phone with someone and they cross this line, express yourself clearly and respectfully. Facilitate an honest conversation: "I appreciate your interest in my love life, and I know you care for me. However, in future, I won't accept this behaviour. Please respect my boundaries." And if they persist, add further information: "I am going to hang up. Call me when you are ready to respect what I've asked. I love you and don't want this to harm our relationship."

Take the time now to consider what boundaries you have in place and what areas in your life require some. Decide your boundaries and invoke Durga to support you to enforce them to protect your energy and peace.

ESTSANATLEHI

It is time to step into the new. You are the personification of trial by fire, and you can now step into a fresh way of being. Anything is possible.

Estsanatlehi—also known as Changing Woman—is a goddess of the Diné (Navajo) People associated with fertility, the seasons and all life. She is a creator deity. Some versions of her story claim that she created the first man and woman from her skin. Other versions of her mythology proclaim that the first man and woman found her as a baby crying in the clouds and adopted her. Sometimes referred to as White Painted Woman, she is associated with the rites of puberty for young women. Representing the natural order of the universe, Estsanatlehi forever changes yet remains immortal. She grows into an older woman in the winter and starts walking into spring, where she shifts back into a maiden.

Estsanatlehi's Message

To experience your ultimate life, you must be willing to strip yourself to the core and be reborn within this very lifetime. Being born into a world that isn't always welcoming can be challenging. You experience death and renewal from the time you are born. New beginnings always come after destruction and endings. Just as vegetation decays to give way to a new harvest, things in your life have decomposed to make way for fertile new ground. From this fertile soil, new seedlings can burst through the surface, ready to bloom, where previously there was a sense of desolation.

When entering a new reality, it is common to feel unease, confusion, disorientation, or even nothing at all. When you feel like your world is a barren wasteland and you can't sense your future, this can indicate that you are in the phase between death and rebirth. Stagnation lives in this in-between void where everything has died, but the new has not yet taken hold. It may feel like there is no future because right now, it is being remoulded.

Know that it is okay to feel lost, confused or stagnant. This is a necessary phase in life's ongoing process. The phase between endings and new beginnings is essential in your life. The birthing pains are ending, and you are gestating a new self — welcome to spring!

EVE

Evaluate the relationships you hold with women and find opportunities to bring healing to them.

In the Hebrew story of Genesis, Eve was created as a second wife for the first man Adam. Yahweh (God) took one of Adam's ribs, and thus, Eve was born. She was created as a subservient wife in place of the untameable Lilith. Eve gave into temptation when the serpent persuaded her to take a bite of the delicious fruit of the tree of knowledge. Eve convinced Adam to bite the forbidden fruit and became the scapegoat for all good and evil unleashed on the world and the consequences of this duality on humanity. She has been blamed for everything—including the original sin—and thus, women have carried this within their template ever since.

Eve's Message

The state of the relationships with the women in your life—past and present—contribute to your overall connection to the Divine Feminine. Are there connections rife with tension? Notice the areas that could use the salve of healing. It is time to release internalised misogyny from living in a patriarchal society. It is time to heal the mother wounds connected to your matriarchal ancestral line and the karmic entanglements with women within a friendship.

Women have been compared to each other since the dawn of time. This has been ingrained within the collective feminine mind ever since. Many Genesis stories blame women for original sin, introducing the narrative of women competing with each other. The origins of this paradigm can be seen in the story of Eve, the subservient woman brought in to replace the first wife of Adam.

The pitting of women against each other has led to vast distrust and much hurt. Gossip, comparison, backstabbing and jealousy have run rife, causing devastation. It's time now to return to the sisterhood, to bring this outdated pattern out of the shadow and to face the dark feminine. We all—women and men—need to take responsibility for the damage and pain caused and to heal the wounds of our internal divine feminine energy and maternal ancestral lines.

    Surround yourself with women who build you up and want you to succeed. When you are happy, they celebrate your joy, and when you are sad, they feel your sorrow. Be the type of person who builds other women up, encouraging them to shine brightly, knowing that a single candle can light a thousand more without being extinguished. Another woman's fire will not blow yours out — your light will always beam radiantly when reinforced by a deep connection to the Divine Feminine.

FREYJA

Embrace your connection to your divinity through your sexual nature. Find ways to heal wounds, release limiting beliefs and achieve bliss through sexual liberation.

In Norse mythology, Freyja is a Vanir goddess associated with sexuality, love and fertility. Freyja—translating to 'mistress'—is the embodiment of the sexually-liberated woman, unashamedly indulging in sexual pleasure with many gods, regardless of the rumours about her. She is connected with the day of the week, Friday—possibly derived from her name—making her the perfect energy to work with for play. Freyja is heralded as the Queen of the Valkyries, the group of women in charge of deciding who lives and who dies in battle. Wearing a falcon-feathered cloak, enabling her to shapeshift, and riding a chariot drawn by two cats, Freyja is a force to be reckoned with.

Freyja's Message

Sex is one of the most potent forms of pleasure, connection and healing that humans have access to. Sex is healing, life-giving, connecting, powerful and a source of pleasure and joy. The innate nature of the Divine Feminine is to be supremely sexual, so why is it that some modern women struggle so intensely with their sexuality? Today, so many women have trouble opening up to lovers and have difficulty releasing through orgasm. Many have issues with being seen as sexual beings, and some women even find it difficult to discuss the topic openly.

For millennia, women have been stripped of their rights, subjected to assault, lost their babies, and even died from childbirth. Women have been shamed for being sexual, having lovers and being in their wildness.

Over time, sexuality has become shrouded with shaming narratives that have steered it away from its original beauty. Rather than being the ultimate form of love and the most direct connection to the Source, it has become correlated with sin. Liberation from this will require intentional deconstruction of these antiquated ideals.

However, collective healing has begun. The Divine Feminine is currently experiencing a beautiful journey back to her liberated sexual self. To be a part of this journey, reclaim your sexual pleasure and heal the wounds within your sacral chakra.

    To reclaim the powerful, loving, divine, connecting nature of your sexuality, actively own that side of yourself in the ways that feel right to you. Learn about your body and your orgasm. Release the wounded energies from the womb centre or sacral chakra via orgasm. Experiment with cultivating sexual life force energy by retaining orgasm, channelling the energy within, and manifesting by holding a firm intention in mind when you eventually release that orgasm. Reclaim your sexuality to find your pleasure, power, wildness and joy.

HECATE

Decide to move forwards.
Remaining indecisive keeps
you between two timelines.

Known as the Queen of Witches,
Greek goddess Hecate is the
patron of darkness, magic, sorcery,
spells and the night. She is the
Guardian of the Crossroads and is said to be found
where roads meet, accompanied by howling dogs. She
can see in several directions simultaneously — the past,
the present and the future. A triple goddess, Hecate, is
known to usher those going through menopause into
the next phase of life. One of Hecate's mythologies tells
the tale of her assisting Demeter in her search for her
daughter Persephone, guiding her through the pitch-
black night with her illuminating torch.

Hecate's Message

In every moment, you are gifted with the ability to
alter the entire course of your life through the act of
decision-making. The full extent of the fluid nature of
the future is difficult to grasp from a human perspective.
Many possible timelines have the potential to be played

out, depending on what choice you make along your path. Old ones collapse when they no longer make sense, opening to fresh ones in a new direction. It is easy to underestimate the power of what seems like a tiny decision. One seemingly small choice aligned even one degree towards the life you wish to create opens the opportunity for other tiny decisions to be made.

You can continue forwards passively on the default timeline ahead of you—going where life takes you—or you can make a decision and create what you want instead. Making a decision can feel extremely difficult because you are uncertain of the outcome. However, the risk of stepping onto an uncharted path is not as great as the risk of doing nothing.

When you find yourself at a crossroads, you must choose. Not making a choice is a form of decision, leaving you stagnant between two options, floating in and out of two muddled energies. Indecision impedes the Universe from bringing opportunities on a clearly defined path, keeping you in limbo land. Contemplate the decisions that need to be made in your life, spend some time considering the choices available to you and then take any action steps necessary to put you on a clear path forwards.

HINA

Examine the moon's current phase and reflect on its effect on your life, as you are also cyclic by nature.

Hawaiian lunar goddess, Hina, is said to reside within the moon. Originally, she lived on Earth but grew tired of how her husband Maui—a trickster demi-god—and her family treated her. According to Hawaiian legend, she packed up her belongings and left. Hina—also named the Lady in the Moon—was curious about what it was like on the moon and paddled out towards it on her magical canoe until she reached it. Once she arrived, she was struck by the moon's tranquil beauty and decided to stay, becoming a protector of those who travelled at night. Hina is also associated with communication, cycles and feminine strength.

Hina's Message

In the ebony night skies, a full moon bathes the earth in silvery light. A lone wolf howls in the distance while a shepherd uses the lunar glow to illuminate his way as he travels in the cool night breeze. Elsewhere, two lovers separated by distance gaze at the moon's mystical beauty, feeling connected to each other, knowing the other is seeing the same sight. In another distant land, the children of a tribe sit by a fire as an elder recites a fable involving the moon to teach them ethics and morals, while a shaman conducts a ceremony to utilise the power of the full moon to release someone's anguish.

Throughout history, the moon has held various cultural roles and meanings. It's energy has predominantly been associated with femininity, emotions and the unconscious mind. In many cultures, it is a facet of the Divine Feminine, a goddess in her own right.

The moon has been a timekeeper, light source, calendar, compass, tide tracker and source of contemplation and mysticism. Her many powers provide development for humans as they learn about themselves through her ability to be a giant mystic mirror.

Humans have always connected deeply with the moon, and it's time for you to harness your relationship with it now. Make it a habit to track the moon's cycles, and you will learn to honour your sleep, emotions, mood, and energy fluctuations. Being aware of her daily changes will benefit your mind, body, emotions and spiritual self, reminding you of your natural rhythms and allowing you to maximise the benefits of living in a natural cycle — the ebb and flow of life.

INANNA

Apply softness to yourself and those around you. True power does not feel the need to be overly defensive.

Found in the earliest recorded civilisations, Inanna—daughter of Enki, the god of wisdom—is a powerful Sumerian goddess with many aspects shared with those who came after her. Married to Dumuzid, the Mesopotamian god of shepherds and fertility, she is simultaneously the goddess of war and the Queen of Heaven. One of the most powerful stories in her mythology is her descent to the Mesopotamian underworld, Kur, to challenge her sister Ereshkigal's authority. Her power stands the test of time, with more modern goddesses sometimes identified as her. As a goddess of war and heaven, her associations include fertility, sex, war, justice, love, beauty and sensuality.

Inanna's Message

Softness in a harsh world does not only require an open heart but a person who has connected deeply to their inner power. Within the feminine, there are as many facets of energy as gleaming angles in a diamond. So while strength, boldness, wildness and fierceness are necessary, softness is also needed to balance these qualities.

Being gentle requires having sufficient inner fortitude to feel secure enough to let down one's guards of protection. It takes immense bravery, just as much as it would take to walk onto a battlefield, hands in the air, with your weapon at your feet.

Becoming hardened, aggressively defensive and uncompromisingly defiant can come easier in a painful world than a softened touch. A gentle power emerges from an unwillingness to indulge in petty games and unclear boundaries. Instead, you feel powerful enough that you are not easily swayed.

You know that humans contain dark and light and walk a challenging path in a complex and nuanced world. So instead of a snap reaction, you pull up the reserves of your compassion and clearly state your unwillingness to be a part of the cycle because you understand that hurting people is what hurt people do.

The smallest dog barks the loudest because it feels the need to be protected. A large dog can afford to be gentle because it does not fear being powerless. The stronger you become within yourself and in your understanding of why people act out, the greater aligned you will be with the qualities of a large dog, knowing you have a reserve of power and fierceness to call on when needed. It will not be required when you no longer feel threatened.

ISIS

See the possibilities available to you when manifesting by balancing the art of co-creation and surrender.

ISIS

Isis—the daughter of Geb and Nut and the mother of Horus—is the ancient Egyptian goddess of magic associated with fertility, death, sex and wisdom. She has been worshipped for approximately 4500 years. Known as the Lady of Ten Thousand Names, her reach was immense, spreading from Egypt throughout the Near East and across the Mediterranean as far as Greece and Rome. Her temples attracted many initiates, including Mary Magdalene. When her beloved Osiris was murdered, she was so overcome with grief and anger that she created the Nile river with her tears. Using her emotion as a conductor of magic, she tirelessly searched the lands of Egypt until she found him scattered in many pieces. Working together with the god Thoth, she channelled her vast emotion as fuel to conceive their son Horus and bring Osiris back to life. Both became the leading symbols of ancient Egyptian kings — Horus, the manifestation of the sun's light above and Osiris, the undying god of the afterlife below.

Isis' Message

Magic occurs in every moment — each thought, word and action provides you with an opportunity to wield your creative power. Life is like a quilted blanket made of many seemingly minuscule moments built upon each other to create a masterpiece. You do not see the bigger picture until after the creation is complete.

You may not perceive how all the tiny moments correlate, and you may never see from the vantage point of your human mind. Your job is to access the present moment and decide how you will use it for your future advantage and your current joy.

You can unite free will and fate — not casting aside either one for the other. You simultaneously hold feminine and masculine energies — light and dark, action and intuition, and creation and surrender.

Manifestation through co-creation is the most potent form of transformation. Your capacity to understand that you are co-creating with others and the Universe is how you hold your power.

Combining the art of surrender and creation is a powerful manifestation tool. When you make a decision, you then surrender to the decisions of others involved and what emerges from the co-creation.

Once the decisions have been made in unison—and everything settles as a result—you can spring back into action. Manifestation requires the skills of both actively creating and passively surrendering. This is surrender and creation in action — balancing the contributions of others and the Universe with your plans.

    Move forwards using your knowledge of co-creation to manifest your highest potential joy.

IXCACAO

Nourish your body, mind and soul through deep rest and nourishment. Slather yourself in self-care to bring restoration in a world full of burnout.

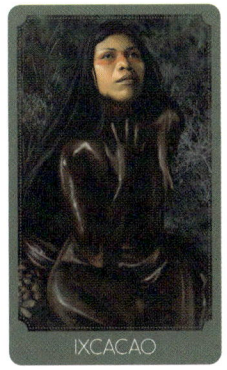

Often referred to as the chocolate goddess, Ixcacao is one of the deities featured in the origin stories of the Mayan civilisation. Since the time of creation itself, Ixcacao has been associated with fertility, the earth, agriculture and the cacao bean. Cacao was incredibly important to the Aztecs; they believed that the gods discovered it within a sacred mountain. Cacao beans were so important that they were used as currency. Cacao was touted as a divine drink that nourished so deeply that it fought off famine. Ixcacao's primary role at the beginning of Mayan culture was to assist in the nourishment of crops, prevent starvation and ensure her people's survival.

Ixcacao's Message

Many modern ideologies surrounding diet and success perpetuate a restriction mentality, whereas you will flourish and thrive with a replenishment mentality. For too long, people have been held to unrealistic and rigid expectations that make them feel guilted into regimented, restrictive ways of living. These ideals are delivered to us daily as we are bombarded with overly-photoshopped images of slim healthy people, diet programs, wellness products and services declaring false promises of achieving unattainable goals.

Liberate yourself from these antiquated regimes based on punishment now. The sheer energy of penalty and guilt stand on the opposite side of the spectrum of nourishment and pleasure. It's time to step into habits that nourish all of you instead.

Make it a daily practice to be aware of the patterns that prevent you from feeling strong and replenished. Nourishment is a way for you to fall deeply into your divine feminine energy, to be provided for and to be in a state of receiving.

Look at food as a way to provide you with emotional satiation and nourishment for your body. Another way to replenish yourself is to do things not only for productivity but also for rest. Rest is a form of action as it allows your body and nervous system the space it needs to reset, regenerate and restore. If you take time for your health, you can avoid needing to take double the time later to recover from an illness.

Tap in to the frequency of nourishment to deeply replenish the energetic stores of your mind, body, spirit and soul. Find every available opportunity to cherish yourself and lavish yourself with nourishment in the forms that feel most blissful to you.

IXCHEL

Be gentle with yourself as you experience the ups and downs of the healing process.

As the Mayan goddess of healing, medicine, water, weather, the moon and the arts, Ixchel is said to have watched over the creation of humanity. Her name translates as Lady Rainbow, and she fulfilled her role as a fertility goddess by sending rain to the earth to aid the crops. She wears a serpent in her hair, symbolising her healing abilities and wisdom. In Mayan culture, snakes are revered and seen as powerful symbols of fertility, renewal and rebirth. As a moon goddess, Ixchel is often depicted in either of the three aspects of the goddess—Maiden, Mother or Crone— to represent the moon's changing phases. In some representations of Ixchel, she is depicted as an evil crone with many shadow aspects — an acknowledgement of the dark side of the feminine.

Ixchel's Message
Embark on a healing journey because you deserve it, not because you are broken and need fixing. You are not

healing to become a better version of yourself but rather to love the parts of you that you sometimes don't deem deserving of love.

Healing occurs in an upwards spiral pattern through three stages — blockage, integration and flow. It may seem counterintuitive, but when you have experienced a phase of spiritual awakening, you can experience a period of feeling heavy afterwards. Anything within you that no longer fits the new vibration must be released. This change then sparks an integration phase that allows for flow and room for more energy to surface.

Healing is not all positivity, rainbows and rays of sunshine. Levelling up can lead to a deepening of the ebbs and flows that you experience. Healing to feel only happiness and pleasure is not attainable. It does not mean that you no longer feel heavy emotions — instead, it makes you better at *feeling*. It doesn't take away your problems; it helps give you the ability to solve them with resilience and a clear mind.

Instead of taking away the darkness, you will learn to be no longer afraid of the dark. Ultimately, you will enjoy happiness and lightness when it occurs and appreciate the contrast offered. Satisfaction is not to be clung to. It is to be enjoyed in this moment while it lasts, with a sense of peace that comes from leaning into life cycles.

JOAN OF ARC

Find your voice and speak up to communicate your needs and your opinions.

As the saviour of France, Joan of Arc is one of the most renowned heroines of all time. At the tender age of eighteen, Joan, living in medieval France, felt that she heard the message of God speaking to her. She took on the mission to lead France to victory in the long-standing war with England. Standing tall in her self-belief, she enlisted the faith of Prince Charles, and the peasant girl became a military leader and warrior. With Joan of Arc's involvement, the French royal army had their first battle success in the siege of Orleans. In 1431, Joan—at nineteen—was tried for witchcraft and heresy and ultimately burned at the stake.

Joan of Arc's Message

We tend to leave things unsaid out of an assumption that the other person innately understands our perspective, needs or wants. However, this assumption is the cause of much unnecessary misunderstanding and confusion in interrelationships.

Without speaking your needs, the possibility of them being met is next to nil. Becoming a master communicator will completely transform the ease with which you interact with the people around you and the satisfaction of your needs. You deserve to have your needs met in spades.

The energy that keeps many intuitive people from feeling able to speak up and use their voice is the persecution energy that stifles their throat chakra. The magical person bears the cross of repression and persecution so profoundly that they can struggle to find their voice through the pain. Thankfully, the time on Earth for persecution is slowly ending.

You are a soul in tune with healing; like the healers, mystics and shamans burned at the stake, dragged through the streets by their hair or drowned in rivers, you deeply feel the remnants of persecution's pain. These magical people were cast out of their communities by those who did not understand how to connect with their power, the earth or the Divine.

It is time for this pain within your somatic memory to be cleansed. As you work through your persecution energy and throat chakra blocks in conjunction with researching and practising communication skills, your voice will become clearer and stronger before you know it.

KALI MA

Be willing to walk away from all in your life that no longer serves you. Something must die for something new to be reborn.

KALI MA

Kali Ma—the dark mother—is the all-powerful Hindu goddess associated with destruction, death and endings. Regarded as the most potent embodiment of Shakti, she carries a sword of truth and a severed head to symbolise the destruction of ignorance and detachment from ego. Often feared for her unrelenting, fierce nature, Kali Ma is like the stern mother who will tell you the truth, although difficult, because she cares. She stands in the middle of a storm, utterly unafraid because she knows the purpose destruction serves. As the master of time, change and death, she will strip you down, knowing that you will be rebuilt from the ground up, creating a better version of you.

Kali's Message

Sometimes, you will have to choose to let go of something even when you don't want to or don't feel ready to accept that it is in your best interest. Seeking opportunities to detach intentionally will help you learn the skill for the times you feel the Universe is forcing your hand.

Take an inventory of the things you feel the strongest attachment to and put a plan in place to find a way to let go of them, even temporarily. For example, if you find comfort in not leaving your home town, arrange a trip to broaden your horizons. Or if you find comfort in driving your car to get around, practise walking or taking public transport for a week. Getting comfortable with these temporary intentional detachments will assist you in starting to face the more important things you need to address.

Embrace your inner phoenix. When the phoenix knows it is time to burn down to the ashes, even the nest she is in burns to the ground. It takes bravery to allow elements of your life to burn to the ground and walk away. This could include relationships that you stay in out of comfort even though deep inside you know it is time to move on; or jobs that have become barren of joy, but you continue out of security even though it crushes your soul.

Recognise where your identity has merged with something that is not truly a part of you and then release it. Make a conscious decision to become a master of the advanced soul lesson of detachment. Let go and be ready to hold yourself through the grief, loss and fear of the unknown. Let go and feel everything crumble around you, knowing you will be rebuilt once more.

LADY OF THE LAKE

You are an alchemist. Turn your pain into power. Dive inwards to retrieve hidden aspects of yourself.

The Lady of the Lake is one of the most revered figures in Avalonian mythology. According to legend, she lives in a castle under the lake surrounding Avalon. She is the ever-powerful enchantress most recognised as the being who emerged from the lake's depths to present King Arthur with his sword Excalibur. She has become one of the prominent and significant examples of female magic. Her wondrous tales of wild feminine energy—untamed and unapologetic—range from adopting Sir Lancelot as her child to locking an enchanted Merlin in a tree to her ability to manipulate the element of water. The Lady of the Lake is a powerful example of women tapping back into their power and magic.

Lady of the Lake's Message

Conducting alchemy of the soul is similar to Lady of the Lake diving deep into the murky unknown waters to retrieve Excalibur to present to King Arthur. Those brave enough to leave the stability of the land behind and enter the depths of their metaphorical internal lake will reap the rewards of spiritual transformation.

There are different ways to handle the pressures life places upon you. You can succumb to these and become bitter and defeated, or you can come out the other side stronger than you ever thought possible. Just as the alchemist can change a lump of coal into gold, you can transmute your pain to power. For example, if you lose your job, you can pick yourself up, dust yourself off and apply for your dream job. If you experience a breakup in a relationship, you can allow your heartbreak to lead you to a path of healing and independence. If you have a falling out with your friendship group, you can actively seek a new support network more aligned with the current version of you.

Alter your perspective to view the parts of your life that seem like cold lumps of coal and turn them into the source of your transformative power. Instead of feeling the weight of life's hardness, start to feel excitement at the possibilities presented to you via these weighty challenges.

Life's pressures can lead you to retrieve hidden pieces of your soul and integrate them into your being. Dive deeply into the dark lake of your unconscious mind, unearth these shining pieces of you and bring them back to shore.

LILITH

Liberate yourself from the antiquated notions placed upon you by society. Expectations and shame can only be placed upon you if you allow it.

Lilith is an important figure in some Sumerian and Hebrew traditions. In some texts, she is portrayed as the first woman created from the same earth as Adam. It is said that when Adam desired subservience from her, she was ruthless in her defiance. Why should she be subservient when she was created as an equal. In some versions of Lilith's story, she fled the Garden of Eden to live out her days by the Red Sea. Other versions claim she was expelled. Either way, Lilith never returned and was replaced as Adam's wife by Eve. Lilith symbolises liberation for the feminine: unafraid to start again and leave everything behind out of total assurance of one's birthright to power and her place in the world.

Lilith's Message

It is time to break free of any shackles holding you back from living your life as a sovereign being. In what ways have you kept yourself small? Are these due to antiquated belief systems suppressing your wild, feminine energy?

During this time, you are experiencing life like a snake shedding its skin — shedding old versions of yourself, old ways of thinking, limiting beliefs and outdated societal structures keeping you from freedom. Through the liberation of these old skins, you are stepping more and more into renewed empowerment. Liberate yourself—in all ways—over and over, again and again.

A powerful way to liberate yourself is to become aware of the usage of the word 'should'. Catching yourself expressing what you 'should' be doing is a golden opportunity to notice areas where you are repressing yourself. The energy behind the word 'should' is loaded with burden and falsified requirements.

Ask yourself why you feel the energy of 'should' instead of 'want'. Is it because you think you must do 'this thing' because of societal norms? Or is it something that you want for yourself and your life? You are the only person who can allow an expectation to be put on you. Nobody can expect you to behave a certain way unless you invite and comply with that expectation.

    The greatest form of liberating yourself is to make a conscious effort not to abandon yourself. If someone does not choose you, it is always an opportunity to choose yourself. Return to yourself, and you will find freedom.

MA'AT

Forgo comfort in favour of embracing the hard truths you may have been avoiding.

Ma'at, daughter of Ra, is the ancient Egyptian goddess of truth, balance and justice. Married to the god of wisdom, Thoth, Ma'at was highly esteemed for her role as the conductor of the ceremony of judgement for the dead. In folklore, Ma'at would await the newly deceased, ready to weigh their hearts against her feather of truth on the scale of justice. Her judgement would dictate whether the heart was light enough to allow entrance into the afterlife, accompanied by Osiris, the ancient Egyptian god of death and resurrection. Working with Ma'at can help restore equilibrium and an understanding of self and morality through her seven principles — truth, justice, harmony, balance, order, propriety and reciprocity.

Ma'at's Message

Becoming a cycle breaker holds unimaginable levels of power. It allows you to become a force to be reckoned with. Today you are being asked to face the scales of justice and let yourself see areas that you may have previously been looking at through rose-tinted glasses. Humans naturally tend to tell themselves narratives that cover them in a blanket of perfect illusion. We tell ourselves what we want to hear to keep us in a perpetual delusion that feels comfortable to avoid experiencing the pain of the truth. We tell ourselves comforting lies, such as our childhood wasn't that bad or the person not treating us right will change.

On the surface, it appears to be easier to live in a comfort zone, but it is only less painful in the short term, not in the long run. Staying in the illusion can cause greater pain as disillusionment builds and grows. It encapsulates a stagnant timeline devoid of growth and change.

Ripping off the band-aid in one fell swoop gets you to a painless horizon quicker than ripping it off one tiny bit at a time, staying in a drawn-out pain cycle. Becoming comfortable with being uncomfortable will allow you to rid yourself of the old and build brand new behaviours and beliefs more aligned with a brighter future.

Take ownership of your ability to change your behaviour and the perspectives and beliefs you hold. It takes deep introspection and bravery to be completely honest with yourself about certain aspects of your life. However, when you become an expert at practising self-reflection, you no longer fall victim to repeating the same cycles and feeling like life is happening to you without your control.

MARY MAGDALENE

Reflect on the lessons your relationships bring into your life to maximise the catalyst they may be for you.

Mary of Magdala is the epitome of the repressed Divine Feminine. Although she has been given many roles and names throughout time, for the most part, her story has been kept out of the history books. Mary has been called a prostitute and a sinner and has not been adequately portrayed for the role she played during the time of Yeshua. In modern times, it is speculated that she was Yeshua's wife and one of his most devout disciples. She showed devotion by anointing him with spikenard oil and washing his feet with her hair. It is said that Mary was one of the first to witness Yeshua after his resurrection. She is influential in the return of the Divine Feminine through teaching and leadership. Her story will be told.

Mary Magdalene's Message

Just as souls come in infinite divine forms, so do soul connections and relationships. All relationships are sacred as each is an embodiment of teacher and student. The container of a relationship is our grandest catalyst for growth, learning and spiritual maturation. Even though all relationships are sacred, staying in a relationship with poor treatment is not advised, nor is it healthy. Sometimes growth and learning occur from walking away.

Throughout your lifetime, relationships will show up in various forms, such as mother, child, friend or through different types of lovers. The three components of love—passion, commitment and intimacy—allow for endless combinations of expression. Lovers experiencing the fiery lightning bolt of passion flying between them. A long-time married couple with infinite commitment who have grown together throughout a lifetime of shared memories. Or a dear soul mate with open vulnerability and emotional intimacy.

At different stages of life, a particular flavour of love satisfies a need or a lesson. Perhaps at one stage, a passionate soul connection comes into your life as a lover to help you heal and grow your sexuality. At another point on your journey, a loving, soothing partner enters as a gentle soul mate relationship to ease open your heart. Then there are the karmic connections who come steamrolling into your life to serve as a kind of microscope — rife with emotion and growth, sometimes teaching you the most about your relationship with yourself, causing you to choose yourself when they don't.

Journey forward knowing that each of your relationships—the good, the heart-breaking and the frustrating—are leading you to the mastery of the all-encompassing, power-loaded *agape*, the selfless, unconditional love that helps people to forgive, respect and serve one another, day in and day out.

MEDUSA

You are profoundly and unequivocally acknowledged for the hurt you have been dealt in your life. Allow these words to hold you in love and soothe you as you are seen in your pain.

Medusa is commonly known as the Greek monster who turns men to stone with just one stern gaze. Before she was a Gorgon—a snake-haired winged female from Greek mythology—she was a beautiful maiden. While she served as a priestess of Athena, Medusa was raped by Poseidon, the sea god, within the walls of one of Athena's temples. Instead of being protected and cared for after the abuse, Medusa incurred the wrath of Athena, who cursed her to become the monster she is now known as. Medusa is the epitome of the archetype of a villain borne from victimhood. Not only was she raped by a man, but a fellow woman also banished her.

Medusa's Message

Through these words, you are acknowledged, seen and validated. You are not being asked to do anything and are not given solutions or a higher perspective. In this moment, you are seen for the human you are and the pain you are experiencing.

Take a moment to put your hand over your heart and acknowledge the unfairness of the pain you have been subjected to in your life. Allow yourself to feel whatever is at your core, whether anger at the atrocities accosted to you and others, betrayal of being hurt by people who were meant to love you, or any other injustices experienced.

Today, you are not being asked to let go or forgive. Instead, this is a time to acknowledge your grief, despair or sadness. Sometimes part of a healing path is stopping for a moment and allowing yourself to feel your victimhood and accept that people can be utterly cruel to each other.

For now, it is essential to put aside any spiritual perspectives you may have been told about manifestation or soul contracts. To honour yourself and tap in to your pain, you may have to acknowledge that you—as a human—did not choose to be hurt.

Sometimes healing requires you to see the higher perspective of your existence, knowing that it serves a purpose — but this is not one of those times. You would not tell a small child that they asked to be hurt before coming into this life or that they need to be strong. Give yourself the same gentleness and allow a moment of silent solace for the hurt parts of you. This is the healing.

MUSSO KORONI

Sit with the discomfort of feeling alone. Being human can feel incredibly difficult, and learning to apply the salve of love to the primal wound of separation is paramount.

According to the origin story of the Bambara of Africa, Musso Koroni was the first woman to be created. She is the voice of the void and the first wife on Earth. Bemba, the creator god, generated the first-ever set of twins, Musso Koroni and Pemba. The pair left Heaven, creating consciousness by breaking the bond between heaven and earth and populating the planet. Musso Koroni disliked Pemba so much that she decided to forsake him and flee. She wanders the planes of the earth to this day, causing sadness and disorder within humans wherever she goes. The first person to have felt the loneliness of separation, it is theorised that all human beings that have come after her carry this aspect of her within them.

Musso Koroni's Message

Loneliness is a symptom of humanity's primal wound and can be unrelentingly cruel. Separation, the wound embedded within humanity, is a vital part of the earthly experience.

The moment of birth is highly jarring, being ejected from the warm confines of the womb and becoming entirely dependent. This experience is exactly what it feels like to be torn from our Source and to plummet down the layers of consciousness to a world of duality. The feeling of separation experienced exists so that you can journey back to your ability to tap into the Source.

A significant element of the journey back to Source is an inward one. Although this return journey can be experienced via relationships, anyone who has felt deep loneliness while lying next to their partner at night will know that the antidote to feeling separate is not reliance on another. You can feel utterly alone within a relationship and yet completely whole and happy single. Loneliness has little to do with being surrounded by people or being content alone — it is felt deep within.

Relationships can play their part in conjunction with the deep inner work of self-love and sitting with the pain of separation. From a human level, you are a social being biologically driven to connect with others, whether through family, friendship or romantic connections. From a spiritual level, relationships are your biggest healer and teacher. You will have time to experience both sides of the equation — time alone and time partnered; neither is better than the other.

    Single or partnered, take the time to stop running from the pain of separation and pause for a moment to place your hand over your heart. Take a steady breath, knowing that the feeling of connection will come your way.

NYX

Take a walk in the realm of the shadow to face what lurks in the darkness of your psyche.

According to Greek mythology, Nyx is the personification of the night. As the Greek goddess of the night, Nyx is acknowledged as one of the primordial gods who oversaw the dawn of creation itself. Containing light and shadow aspects, Nyx is said to play either a good or bad role for humanity, depending on what she chooses at that moment. The myth is that she intimidated even the most powerful god, Zeus. Toted as the only goddess he ever feared, Zeus was threatened by the fact that Nyx was older and stronger. Nyx, representing the unknown, fear and mystery, lived in Tartarus, the deep abyss used as a prison of torment and suffering for the Titans.

Nyx's Message

It can be terrifying to contemplate wandering into the shadowy realms of the darkness when you've learned that focusing on the negative is manifesting it into your reality. However, fearing the dark and avoiding it does not dull what is lurking underneath; it makes it scream louder into the void.

The shadow is like a small child screaming out for attention. Until you can wrap your arms around the darkest parts of yourself and others with loving acceptance, it will feel like you are out in the cold instead of under the sun's warming rays. We have aspects of ourselves that have been disowned, hidden, rejected or unseen. Many elements can form parts of our shadow sides, such as emotions, personality traits, sexuality, needs, desires, beliefs, thoughts and traumas. There are emotions that, at some point, were too difficult to feel—such as grief or anger—or that you think you shouldn't feel, such as jealousy. Other emotions may have felt difficult to handle because survival mode kicked in or were explained away with the mind. Other disowned parts of you come from how you learned to stay safe as a child.

It is essential to allow the unconscious parts of you that your conscious ego does not identify with to come to the surface. If ignored or intellectualised, these emotions don't magically disappear but instead get pushed down deep into your subconscious mind, playing out from the background.

Are you ignoring your needs to appease others, acting tough or masking vulnerability with a cold demeanour or stuffing down leadership qualities after being told you were bossy? It's time to change this. Every single fragment of you deserves to be seen, loved and held. Take a walk into the shadowy realms of your darkness and find yourself returning to life.

OYA

Remember how powerful you are and decide in this moment to call back any power you may have had stripped away and stand with your head held high.

In the Yoruba religion of West Africa, Oya is esteemed as one of the seven most powerful Orishas. Daughter of Yemoja, Oya—meaning 'she tore'—is the goddess of weather due to her ability to wield the elements. Associated with wind, tornadoes and lightning, she uses these elements to create violent storms. Also referred to as the Mother of Nine, it is said that for each of the nine babies she miscarried, another stream of the Niger River was born. A warrior queen and a guardian of the realm between life and death, Oya—with her connection to the element of air—represents the aspect of the cycle of life and death, the life found in a breath of fresh air.

Oya's Message

In a world that has vilified those who have stood firm in their power, it can feel intimidating to put your own on display for fear of persecution. Is it possible that fear and beliefs about strong, fiery people keep you from acknowledging your true nature? People in their power can be seen as selfish, brazen and threatening when they are unwilling to comply with what others want.

Make decisions based on what feels most nurturing to you, not out of old people-pleasing habits. There may be a subconscious part of you that has grown up feeling that your worth comes from caretaking, but from this moment forward, you do not have to do anything to prove your worthiness. Let go of what others think of you while you change your people-pleasing ways. If someone expects you to overgive, their opinion is not relevant.

Until you get the hang of this, you may have to fake it until you make it by asking yourself, "What would someone who is fully in their power choose to do in this moment?" Empowerment can look like opposite things for different people. Even for you, it can look like other things at various stages of your path. Right now, saying no to going out socialising with your friends might feel like a powerful choice, but in a month, it might be the very thing you need to be in your power.

The ultimate form of harnessing your power can simply be saying no without following up with a reason. You are not required to prove to another that your no is valid.

Be proud of your personal power and use it to benefit you and everyone around you. Trust your true nature and your ability to make wise, powerful choices. Don't fear the opinions of others, and let your undaunted self flow like a breath of fresh air.

PACHAMAMA

Forgive yourself and others. The process is not instant. Take one step at a time along the winding path of forgiveness.

Pachamama—translating to Mother Earth—is the ancient Incan goddess honoured by the Indigenous People of the Andes mountains. A theocratic society, the Inca civilisation lived from the 1400s to the 1500s. Their religion consisted of deities who were the force of various aspects of nature. Pachamama was the physical embodiment of Mother Earth, with many of her depictions showing her form as the mountains. She is associated with fertility, the seasons, earthquakes and harvesting. With the ability to cause earthquakes, Pachamama not only fulfils a nurturing motherly role for the world but also represents a formidable force with the power to cause destruction. Mother to Inti, the sun god, and Mamakilla, the moon goddess, Pachamama is a powerful source of life and nourishment.

Pachamama's Message

The burden carried with you after experiencing pain caused by another can grow over time. Just as holding a large rock may feel easy at first, the longer you hold it, the heavier it feels. It is time to put the rock down. When you are carrying the burden of resentment, the first step of the journey is to begin. That is the thing about forgiveness; it all starts with the choice to forgive.

Wanting to forgive is not enough. It is not achieved with one decision; it is a timeline that opens before you when the initial decision is made. To the hurt parts of you, it can feel like a slap to the face to be asked to forgive. The hurt parts of you do not want to because the resentment feels like a validation of the pain caused. When this occurs, remind yourself that while the pain is validated, forgiveness is because you deserve peace, not because the pain was justified. Forgiveness is an inside job, not for the other person but for you.

Resistance to releasing resentment indicates that there is repressed pain to feel. There would be no resistance if there were no more pain to face. During this part of the process, it can be helpful to temporarily put aside the call to see things from a higher perspective, to gift yourself space to lean into the feeling of being the victim. It may feel counterintuitive to forgive through feeling like a victim, but it is necessary for the movement of that emotion. You will not remain there forever. One day you will realise that you have worked through so much and held yourself through it so firmly that forgiveness has arrived naturally, at the right timing.

PANDORA

Look at your unfavourable circumstances and see if there's a possibility that they could be good luck in some way.

In the Greek pantheon, Pandora is the first woman on Earth. Before humanity, Gods and Titans reigned solo. Prometheus defied Zeus by gifting humanity the element of fire, which was intended only for Gods. Zeus decided that all of humanity should be punished for Prometheus' defiance. Pandora was created with beauty, wisdom, kindness and curiosity. Using the trait of curiosity to her disadvantage, Zeus gave Pandora a box to take to Earth, forbidding her to open the contents. Pandora's curiosity overcame her, and she unwittingly unleashed evil on the planet. When all evil was released from the box, she opened it one last time, and hope emerged, swirling out in beautiful bursts of light after all the darkness.

Pandora's Message
Looking from outside of the earthly perspective, situations you are in can be seen as innately neutral —

neither good nor bad. However, the human mind creates a negative or positive attachment to experiences. This is okay because we live in a realm based on duality for a reason — to experience all forms of human reality, including darkness and hope. Hope only exists because the darkness does.

Is there a situation that you are viewing as unfavourable that could be seen through the lens of hope? Maybe you just got rejected for a job offer and feel unsupported by the Universe. Perhaps the person you are dating has suddenly ghosted you leaving you broken-hearted. Maybe you are down to the last ten dollars in your bank account and feel fear bubbling up in your chest. Your feelings are valid, and you are invited to feel the emotion attached.

But what if this situation is not bad luck but good luck instead? What if you were denied that job because the Universe knew it would make you miserable and keep you stuck on an unfulfilling path? What if that lover ghosting you is a blessing in disguise to keep you from delving into an unhappy relationship? What if having ten dollars left motivated you to face your lack mentality and led you to step into your life purpose?

Take an inventory of your current circumstances and come up with a way to hold hope in your heart for an outcome that benefits you, even if all you see is darkness.

PERSEPHONE

Use your mind and logic to help you find a resolution to the situations you currently find yourself in. Feel the pull of your heart and bring your dreams to fruition using your logic.

A member of the Greek pantheon, Persephone is a maiden goddess of spring. Daughter of Zeus and Demeter, Persephone is also known as the Queen of the Underworld. Taken by Persephone's immense beauty, Hades decided he wanted to marry her. He abducted her as she picked flowers in the woods with her maidens and dragged her to the underworld. Tricked by Hades into eating six pomegranate seeds, Zeus ruled that Persephone would be required to live six months of the year in the underworld. For the other six months of the year, she would be granted the freedom to walk again over the earth. Her return to the world marks the beginning of spring.

Persephone's Message

The mental realm can often be shunned in favour of solely following the heart and emotions. This is like throwing the baby out with the bath water.

Transcendence is the ability to surrender to the flitting between the higher and lower perspectives — the vehicle to achieve this is the mind. The trick is using the faculties of the mind in conjunction with your emotional guidance, intuition and heart space. Every tool can have limitations. Combining all the tools you have been gifted bypasses those limitations while maximising the benefits.

Using only logic without heart-led intuition is unbalanced, yet the same is valid for living entirely in emotions. Taking into consideration the direction your heart is pulling you in but using your mind, logic and reason to get you there is the most effective technique to achieve your intentions.

Your mind can assist you in discerning and analysing situations, knowing when to proceed with caution and come up with grounded ideas and steps to help you achieve your heart's desires. The mind is your gateway to your subconscious and is a part of your multifaceted nature.

It can feel frustrating when your mind flits between different opinions and thoughts. Listen to the variety of information ebbing and flowing to gain access to the various aspects of yourself. You don't have to come to one thought or one definitive answer. Instead of giving yourself inner turmoil by stifling all thoughts, harness them as a resource to gain access to the information flowing to you.

    Appreciate your mind and consciously use it and your logic to help usher your heart's deepest wishes into reality with intent and intelligence.

QUAN YIN

Feel your emotions instead of repressing them. Thinking does not release them. Instead, sit with the feeling itself, even if it's uncomfortable.

The one who hears the world's cries, Quan Yin, is the goddess of compassion and mercy in Chinese mythology. She is a *bodhisattva*, meaning that she has forgone nirvana and vowed to stay on Earth until each human is enlightened and is no longer in the cycle of reincarnation. A soothing, nurturing presence, Quan Yin brings peace to those suffering along their path of duality. It is said she answers each prayer she hears, sometimes taking on an unassuming form to offer help in inconspicuous ways. Her mythology says that she tried so hard to understand the needs of all who suffer that her head split into eleven, and she grew a thousand arms.

Quan Yin's Message

Without emotions, the experience of being a human would not be an experience at all, yet people fight their feelings all the time. Emotions connect you to the highest of joys and the deepest of pain. Switching off from the pain dulls the ability to feel all emotions, including pleasure. And it isn't even possible to avoid the effects of the pain anyway. The best way to embrace the experience of being human is to treat the emotional realm as just that — a realm separate from the mind.

Although there is a link between thoughts and emotions, they are not the same. They are each a separate realm that exists simultaneously. Therefore, you cannot process emotions purely by attempting to cognise them. Understanding why the emotion is there is not always productive and can impede your ability to drop into the feeling. You do not always get to know what that emotion is tapping into — it could be unprocessed childhood trauma or past-life energies lingering in the subconscious. Acknowledge it is there, and process the emotion regardless of where it originated.

Emotions are processed by dropping into the body through deep breaths and noticing the sensations occurring in your physical body, allowing them to be, and being okay with sitting in the discomfort. Rejecting the emotion can lead to reactive behaviour, loss of inner peace and decisions made from an unclear mind.

    Considering we are emotional beings, humans are still immature on the evolutionary scale in terms of emotional intelligence and skill. Focus on learning about your emotions. Let yourself feel and regulate your emotions by implementing breathing practices and other valuable tools, such as meditation. See your relationships and quality of life dramatically shift. Be present with your feelings, be aware of them, and be knowledgeable and they will not rule you.

QUEEN MAYA

Honour the second stage of the goddess in the form of the Mother, who turns the lessons of maidenhood into life itself and begins to embody the wisdom of the Crone.

In Buddhist legend, it is said that Gautama Buddha's mother, Queen Maya of Shakya, foresaw his arrival. One morning twenty years into her marriage, she awoke to tell her husband, King Suddhodhana, of her prophetic dream foretelling the birth of a future son. In her dream, four devas took her to Lake Anotatta. After swimming in the lake, a six-tusked white elephant holding a lotus flower appeared and entered her right side. Her intuition told her that she would become pregnant with an incredibly important son. She is the epitome of the power a mother holds, even before she falls pregnant. In 563 BCE, she died shortly after giving birth to Prince Siddhartha and became reborn in the *Tusita* heaven (one of six *deva worlds* where the *bodhisattva* dwelt).

Queen Maya's Message

To honour the goddess is to honour the Mother. The Mother takes the pain gathered on her voyage as the Maiden and turns it into power. She knows who she is and is unapologetic for it. Not seeking the approval of others, she nourishes herself.

A force to be reckoned with, she is bold, unyielding and welcomes the energy of responsibility, wearing it like a crown. Entering the motherhood stage of the goddess requires an internal death of the Maiden. Not entirely, for part of her is integrated deeply within the Mother's core. But the formative version of her must go through a transformation — space must be made.

The joys of motherhood are often spoken about, but the shadow side is not acknowledged enough: the difficulties and the grief of the Mother losing her maiden-self. Thinking she had it all figured out, the Maiden enters motherhood only to become humbled by the force of her creation. Once free to run wild and to journey as she wished, the Maiden has no choice but to take on responsibilities and make way for her sizzling power and intuition.

The Mother's power is tangible because she bore witness to the creation of life, sometimes born through her physically and sometimes through creating a project as if plucking something from thin air like magic. She can be a mother to those she birthed or a mother to those around her who crave a source of nurturing.

If the Maiden represents the birth of new beginnings and the Crone represents fulfilment and death, the Mother represents everything between birth and death — life itself.

QUEEN OF SHEBA

You are being reminded that you do not need to do anything to be deemed worthy of receiving. You are safe to tap into the abundant flow of the universe now, just as you are.

The Queen of Sheba is known for her quest to seek wisdom, first referenced in the Hebrew bible. She is referenced in several religious texts as a wealthy monarch who journeyed to Israel to meet with King Solomon after vigorously questioning his wisdom and testing his knowledge by asking him a series of riddles. The ruler of the kingdom of Sheba, she arrived in a camel-drawn caravan and presented the king with riches. Legend says that her gifts included 120 tablets of gold, precious stones and a variety of spices — a sign of great abundance at the time. It is believed that the Queen of Sheba stayed in Jerusalem for six months, soaking in wisdom before returning home.

Queen of Sheba's Message

Many try to gain from a frenzied state, overgiving in an attempt to feel deserving of getting. However, harried energy is not conducive to receiving, and overgiving generally leads to more of the same. Becoming centred and in tune with your natural ebbs and flows due to your cyclic nature can lead you to tap into the frequency of receiving.

A baby is not born with the requirement to prove its worthiness to receive love, care and nourishment. At what point in your life did you learn that you need to be worthy of receiving? The universe does not require you to give, give and give in order to gift you. You are not required to prove your worthiness by fighting and clawing your way up to a level of deservedness.

The notion of 'being deserving' is unique to humans and has nothing to do with universal law. Your world is so abundant that every person could have their needs and soul desires met without another person missing out.

There can be instances when the universe tries to provide for you, but you say "no". When you say no, you are inhibiting the flow towards you. By saying "yes" as often as possible to opportunities and genuine offers directed at you, you are displaying how receptive you are. Possessing fierce independence can make it difficult to say "yes" to people offering you things. Work on your beliefs surrounding 'being deserving' and feel the flowing of abundance towards you coming from the Source.

SEDNA

You are acknowledged in your despair and pain and are reminded that even though it may not feel authentic, a new dawn will break in time.

Sea goddess, Sedna, is a central figure in Inuit mythology, known as the mother of all marine life. Unhappy with her suitors, Sedna eventually fell for a man who turned out to be a seabird merely masquerading as a man. She left to live with him. After visiting and seeing her living in miserable squalor, her father kills the birdman. As they travelled home in a boat, a flock of birds attacked to avenge the birdman, thus creating giant waves. Sedna's father sacrificed her in an attempt to appease the sea. He cut off each finger one by one as she gripped the boat in terror. Each finger became a various sea creature leading to the origin of Sedna becoming the Mother of the Sea.

SEDNA'S MESSAGE

When you are drowning in a deep ocean of despair, it can feel as if you will never be able to break the surface and take a deep breath of air. When you feel your resolve leaving you and struggle to stay afloat, reach out your hand for support. You do not have to go through this alone. Find professionals or loved ones who can hold space to help you break the surface.

When you are below the surface, it is difficult to remember that anything above the surface exists, yet it does. In the dark night of the soul, you have reached the core of your healing. You have journeyed through the layers keeping you from those gnarly parts of your subconscious and innermost parts of your psyche. The dark night of the soul indicates a breaking down of parts of you that are leaving. It feels like a death because it is one. It is the darkness before the dawn, and in these darkest moments, it is the hardest to grasp a sense of the light.

During the dark night of the soul, productivity is not the top priority, and it will make you feel worse to try and smash huge goals and find them unachievable. Be gentle with yourself if you need lots of rest and comfort; the comfort zone can be a place of healing.

Write a list of ten things that bring you small joys to refer to during this time. Examples include drinking tea from your favourite mug, reading or watching your favourite movie. Find small ways to come to life, such as sitting in the sun, doing yoga, taking a slow walk through nature, conducting your spiritual practice, eating a nourishing meal or consulting with your oracle cards. In time you will emerge from this darkness lighter and at peace.

SEKHMET

Acknowledge the anger that arises within you. Use this anger as fuel to create change.

In ancient Egyptian mythology, Sekhmet—the lion-headed warrior goddess—is synonymous with ferocity, protection, vengeance and war. Daughter of Ra, Sekhmet was renowned as a healer and protector and feared for her destructive nature. Sekhmet was one of several goddesses associated with the Eye of Ra, a feminine counterpart to the ancient sun god. Sekhmet guarded Ra with her spear, which was as deadly as the goddess herself. In one version of her mythology, Sekhmet became so blinded with rage during a battle protecting Ra that she almost killed off all of humanity, only stopping after Ra tricked her into drinking red beer. Waking up from a drunken sleep, Sekhmet saw Ptah—the creator god—for the first time and fell in love, leading her to forget her blood lust.

Sekhmet's Message

There is anger within you that is asking to be acknowledged. You cannot quell the rage in your heart through suppression. Do you hold an internalised belief that anger is not acceptable to exhibit and should be avoided? Comments such as, "Are you on your period?" or being called names, such as "crazy", have led to a negative connotation towards expressing anger. It can feel safer to pretend it does not exist.

Sacred rage is potent and valuable — it protects and creates change. Imagine a fierce lioness protecting her cubs from danger. Her anger gives her the energy to spring into action to keep her cubs safe. Anger is a guiding post to indicate when you or another are being mistreated and when a situation requires attention. Anger can tear down and destroy what needs to go and can also be a function of love. Yes, anger can be loving. If a stranger is mistreating a child, the most loving thing you can do in such a situation is to wield your rage at the perpetrator to protect them.

When imminent danger is not present, find healthy outlets for releasing the built-up pressure. Use your anger as a catalyst for change and stand up for yourself through clear communication and boundaries. Before you approach the situation, take time to feel into it and release anger. Move your body and stomp your feet during a walk as you process your thoughts and feelings. Write an expressive letter and burn it, or scribble on art paper with red and orange crayons as hard as possible. When you feel clear-headed, invoke the guidance that your anger revealed and apply any necessary changes to your life.

SHEELA NA GIG

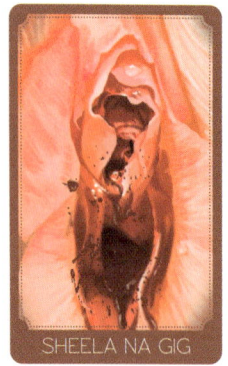

Honour the yoni in all its forms and life cycles, for it contains the gateway to life, wisdom, pleasure and healing.

Sheela Na Gig is the name for sculptures found across Ireland of a grinning crone holding open her vulva with both hands. More than 100 mysterious stone carvings across Ireland have become a powerful symbol representing feminine energy. The name derives from the Norse words *sheila* for woman and *gyg* for a giantess. Long ago, the figures had a grotesque connotation and were viewed as having a lewd connection to the evilness of lust. In modern times, the way this ancient symbol is considered is more aligned with the empowerment and liberation that is occurring with the rise of the feminine.

Sheela Na Gig's Message

The *yoni*—the Sanskrit word for a woman's womb—is the gateway to all life. One can access portals of miraculous opening and newness by honouring the yoni. The womb centre incubates the life cycle, and each woman emulates a mini planet rotating through all four seasons each month.

During a woman's bleeding days, she releases all that no longer serves, just as winter kills off the remnants of the last harvest. The ovulation days are a mini spring, ready for new seedlings to sprout to life. In the days of a hormonal surge, the womb readies itself to destroy the old seedlings reminiscent of a summer storm. The days between the wildness, rest and renewal is autumn. It's a time to appreciate mild weather — not too hot, cold or anything. These are the days to feel free from extremes.

Just as humanity has disconnected from the natural rhythm of Mother Gaia, many of us have disconnected from the power that a menstrual cycle represents. All humans can learn about cycles by looking at the wisdom of the yoni; we can learn about our cyclic nature regardless of who we are or whether or not we menstruate.

Lay down in meditation, tune in and notice what messages are received. For example, painful menstruation cramps may signal a heavy emotion in need of purging. Or, for a male, work with the sacral chakra to gain messages that may help to honour mother nature and the women who influence you. This can bring learning about the cyclic nature of life.

Release old wounds through your orgasm. The dense trauma energies you carry within will be liberated. Hold your desires in mind during orgasm to send a ripple of creative energy to the universe for powerful manifestation.

Honour the yoni, maximise her power, and celebrate who you are.

THE MORRIGHAN

Embrace the element of mystery. Let go of any need to predict the future and enjoy the surprises life brings.

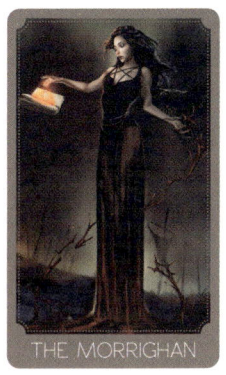

The Morrighan—translating to Phantom Queen—is the Celtic goddess of war, death and destiny. She is a triple goddess associated with life and death — the cycle of life. During times of war, the Morrighan would have premonitions predicting the demise of specific soldiers. Able to turn the tides of battle, she would shapeshift into a raven—a symbol of war and death—and fly over said soldiers' heads to mark their fate. This would either instil fear in the heart of the soldiers or spur them on to fight harder for their life. She is the personification of the dark feminine — vindictive, unyielding and ever-powerful.

The Morrighan's Message
Imagine that you have been handed the book of your life and have sat down and read everything that will happen until your death. You are now privy to each moment you

will experience — the good, the bad and the surprises.

Now, moving forward, imagine living the rest of your life knowing what each moment holds before it happens. Would the surprises feel elating? Would the goals achieved feel thrilling? Would the moments with lovers feel the same if you knew what would happen? Would each joke give you the same belly laugh if you heard it ahead of time?

Mystery is a crucial element of life that humans are lucky to have! You may feel as if you are walking through a maze with a blindfold, not knowing what is in front of you. Although overwhelming, this unknown is what makes life magical. Without it, you would be bored out of your mind with no zest for life and no desire to test your creative ability.

Picture the beauty of having your favourite book from childhood cleared from your mind and re-reading it for the first time. That is the gift you hold — the gift of knowing that some of the most exciting moments of your life are still ahead of you. You have not yet met all the people who will love you and have not yet discovered everything that will bring you joy.

Journey into the mystery — all you need to know is that your story continues. Enjoy the ride.

THETIS

Use your beliefs as stepping stones, never allowing them to be set in stone. Just as you were moulded into your current beliefs, you hold the power to shift out of them.

In Greek mythology, Thetis is revered as the goddess of the sea. She is a sea nymph and Nereid — one of the 50 daughters of the sea god, Nereus. Thetis' abilities include the power to shapeshift and the gift of prophecy. Zeus courted Thetis until it was prophesied that she would bear a son who would be more powerful than his father. Not liking this, Zeus forced her to marry a mortal man, for he did not want her to give birth to his son in fear of the prophecy coming true. A mortal named Peleus was sent to find her. Attempting to evade him, she shapeshifted into various animals, water and fire; he held on tight through all her forms. Ultimately, they wed, and she gave birth to their son, Achilles.

Thetis' Message

Release yourself from the shackles of the external influences that have shaped you. Just as you were moulded into the person you are through your societal influences, you can also develop *from* these patterns or perspectives and become more aligned with your soul.

A belief is a thought repeated so often that it becomes a strongly ingrained system. This system can determine human behaviours and decisions according to the rules dictated by that particular thought. Beliefs are stepping stones along your path, not intended to be set in stone. When you view your thought systems as transitory tools to help you step up to the next portion of your transformation, you will find it easier to question your thoughts.

No belief has to stay a permanent fixture within a person. Deprogramming old ones and creating new ones is not only possible but an essential evolutionary track. Beliefs can become a comfort zone that appeases a part of you seeking soothing. Your brain can become biased towards an idea that makes you feel good and hopeful. This could keep you in toxic relationships and situations that are not geared towards your highest good.

As times change, constructed meanings placed on your surroundings may not apply anymore. Humans before you faced more physical threats and therefore had thought constructs that ran off more of a fear-based survival mode. As a result, many of the thoughts you hold are not meant to belong to you; they were merely passed down to you or absorbed from those around you. Begin to notice when you have a thought that does not make you feel good or does not feel correct. When you notice a belief, challenge it by researching contradictory opinions and keeping an open mind. Allow your mind to shapeshift you into a more appropriate state representing where you are on your journey through a constantly evolving life.

WALU

Connect with your inner child to access your past hurts and current joys.

The mythology of Australia's First Peoples—known as the Dreaming—dates back 65,000 years. It centres around the belief that Earth is continually being created by Dreaming spirits, the physical embodiments of the animals, people and various aspects of the land. In the Dreaming of the Yolngu People, Walu is heralded as Sun Woman. Walu and her daughter Bara journeyed through the sky daily, spreading heat wherever they passed. One day, Walu realised their combined heat not only provided warmth but scorched the lands, making the earth too hot. Walu made the difficult choice to send her daughter back east while she continued journeying to the west to bring back the sun and ensure the earth's fertility persevered.

Walu's Message

Your inner child is the gateway to accessing your deepest emotions and richest joys. Due to the nature of living in a dual plane, designed for learning and growth, humans are like children, even when fully grown — you are here in a state of spiritual amnesia to develop wisdom while seeking your needs to be met, just like your child counterparts.

Unfortunately, adults are not treated with the same level of gentleness and understanding as children. If you struggle to love yourself, practise the art of self-soothing via the medium of the inner child. It can feel easier to speak with your inner child with tenderness when you are not used to positive self-talk.

When you are scared, place your hand over your heart and say, "I know you are scared, and that's okay. I am going to protect you. I'm asking you to be brave and do this scary thing because you will feel so proud of yourself after."

When you feel sad, use words like, "I know you are disappointed and so sad right now, and you are allowed to be. I will hold space for this feeling." Eventually, your inner being will feel so supported that this practice will create an automated feeling of safety. If you did not have a positive childhood home, consciously choosing to become your parent can assist you with working through the pain of the past.

Working with the inner child can also be a direct source of experiencing joy. Part of the experience that Earth has to offer is enjoying the little pleasures of creation. Be present with your inner child, and make time to partake in activities for the sake of joy, not just for productivity.

WHITE BUFFALO CALF WOMAN

You are being called to trust, not that everything will be fine and dandy, but that you will be okay no matter what. Trust yourself, and know that you will overcome whatever life brings you.

Long ago, White Buffalo Calf Woman appeared to the Lakota People of the Great Sioux Nation as a prophetess. She was sent by the Creator when the natives had forgotten how to communicate with Heaven. Discovered by two young hunters, one recognised her sacred energy while the other approached her with ill intent. On approach, White Buffalo Calf Woman covered him with dust, causing him to turn into a pile of bones. The remaining hunter returned to his people, alerting them to her imminent arrival. Appearing from the horizon, she presented her people with a sacred pipe to assist them in bridging the spirit and human worlds.

She taught the Lakota tribe seven ceremonies to use with the pipe to create a harmonious and peaceful future on Earth. As she retreated from the village, she turned into a white buffalo calf.

White Buffalo Calf Woman's Message

It is time to walk forwards on your path holding yourself in strength, relinquishing your concerns for a future that has not yet arrived. The notion of trust is difficult to grasp when, in the past, you have experienced disappointments and hardship.

How can you be expected to have faith when you still feel past bruises? You are not being asked to have blind trust that everything will always be okay. You are being asked to have faith in the process, not that you can guess the outcome or that the result will be pleasant.

Ultimately, you are being asked to have faith in yourself — that you will have your own back, no matter what life throws your way. And even if you get knocked down, you will be okay. You will pause, taking the time to gather yourself before standing up again, and only when you are ready. Allow your mistrust to show you the wounds inside, asking for attention and healing. There is no need to force yourself to trust when you are not ready; listen to what the scared parts of you have to say.

It is human nature to worry; understandably, you

have difficulty trusting when your prior experiences have not always delivered positive outcomes.

When you are asked to hand over your concerns, this is not in any way to indicate that you must tirelessly believe everything will be perfect. Instead, it's to know that specific experiences are being brought onto your path for a reason. Everything you experience is ideal because each moment holds wisdom when you are ready to see it.

Trust cannot be forced; it comes naturally as you build confidence in your ability to navigate unknown terrain.

ABOUT THE AUTHOR

CHRISTABEL JESSICA was raised in Queensland, Australia. At the age of two, she would walk around asking people, "How are you feeling?" and she hasn't stopped since. Her empathy, intuition and desire to learn about humanity and the universe have always been strong.

Christabel studied Early Childhood Education for a few years, then changed to Psychology. Although she loved the content, she didn't finish her degree. Rather, she quit university two days after attending a reiki workshop. From that point, she followed her heart and studied psychic development and intuitive healing, devouring spiritual books and information as if it was her new university course.

While those years of changing course felt confusing, Christabel can now see why she needed to understand how to educate and how to understand the human mind from a scientific and spiritual perspective. She combines these elements in YouTube videos, oracle sets and healing and mentoring sessions to assist those who also feel called to break down the old ways to make way for the new.

Christabel is passionate about providing a safe, healing space for people as they navigate their spiritual journey. Discover more at **www.christabeljessica.com**.

ABOUT THE ARTISTS

Cecilia G.F.

A self-taught illustrator with a degree in art history, Cecilia G.F. uses her knowledge of symbology and art theory to enrich her works with meaning. She draws inspiration from many sources, including music, books, video games and mythology.

Cecilia has collaborated with publishers such as Alethé, Supersonic, Nocturna, Kakao Books and Munyx and worked with clients from all over the world. Some of her best-known cover images are *Clorofilia* by Cristina Jurado (for which she won the Ignotus Award in 2018), *La Compañía Amable* by Rocío Vega, *Sistemas Críticos* by Martha Wells and *El clan sin nombre* by África Vázquez Beltrán.

Discover more of Cecilia's works by connecting with **Thanatosof Nicte** on Twitter, Instagram and Twitch, or **Ceciliagf** on ArtStation.

Cards illustrated by Cecilia G.F.

Anahit, *Athena*, *Baubo*, *Boudicca*, *Brigid*, *Cerridwen*, *Demeter*, *Durga*, *Estsanatlehi*, *Eve*, *Hecate*, *Hina*, *Isis*, *Ixcacao*, *Lilith*, *Musso Koroni*, *Nyx*, *Oya*, *Pachamama*, *Persephone*, *Quan Yin*, *Queen Maya*, *Queen of Sheba*, *Sedna*, *Sheela Na Gig*, *Thetis*, *Walu* and *White Buffalo Calf Woman*.

Dannielle Jones

Whether using oils or digital media, Dannielle Jones likes to incorporate whimsy and reality in every piece she creates. A practising witch, she imbues her paintings with energy and intention for the subject at hand.

Dannielle's work as a freelance illustrator and graphic designer has been recognised and used for book covers, packaging and oracle cards around the world. By working with brands, authors and personal clients, she has turned her passion into a career.

Visit **TheCreativeWitchCo** on Etsy, where Dannielle sells handmade witchy binders, bookmarks, and digital downloads featuring new age themes.

Cards illustrated by Dannielle Jones

Aphrodite, *Artemis*, *Baba Yaga*, *Cleopatra*, *Freyja*, *Inanna*, *Ixchel*, *Joan of Arc*, *Kali Ma*, *Lady of the Lake*, *Ma'at*, *Mary Magdalene*, *Medusa*, *Pandora*, *Sekhmet* and *The Morrighan*.

BLUE ANGEL PUBLISHING

Blue Angel has been illuminating hearts and minds since 1997. Our first major title, *Universal Love Healing Oracle* by Toni Carmine Salerno, is now part of an inspiring catalogue of card sets, books, recordings and more. With thanks to an ever-expanding alliance of writers, artists, editors and designers, Blue Angel has become an industry leader, renowned for crafting beautiful products that bring soulful messages and healing to the world.

A trusted and established network distributes hundreds of Blue Angel titles across the globe. For a list of the major distributors of our English-language editions, please click here. Many of our products are available in other languages, including French, Spanish, Japanese and Dutch. For information on acquiring rights for any of our products contact us here.

Our History

Founded by Toni and Martine Salerno, Blue Angel began life in 1997 as a metaphysical bookstore, art gallery and natural healing centre. The name 'Blue Angel' was Martine's idea, inspired by one of Toni's paintings of Archangel Michael, who is also known as 'the blue angel' or 'blue ray'. Blue Angel Publishing is founded on the unwavering dedication of Toni and Martine and their desire to inspire and help others to help themselves. Blue Angel is a dream realised through the belief that we are all greater than we know ourselves to be, and that we can access a treasure of creativity, intuition and wisdom when we look within. We give thanks to the hundreds, if not thousands, of natural therapists, writers, artists, metaphysical stores, counsellors, reiki practitioners, vibrational healers, mentors, teachers, yoga centres, intuitives, tarot and card readers, and everyone else who contributes to the network of light and love that circles our beautiful planet.

Our Vision

Blue Angel is about embracing life, love and creativity and empowering the soul. We believe words and images can bring light, inspire peace, raise hope and spark joy. We aim to illuminate hearts and minds through beauty, art, music and wisdom, and we invite creators, authors, musicians, healers, believers and dreamers everywhere, to join us. Together, we can help make the world a better place.

Also available from Blue Angel Publishing®

ASTROLOGY ORACLE
Messages from the Stars

JENNIFER FREED, PhD
Artwork by LAILA SAVOLAINEN

Draw on a wealth of astrological wisdom to reveal the primitive, adaptive, and evolving choices available to you in every moment, situation, relationship, and opportunity. Deepen your understanding of the happenings in your world, magnify your impact, and enhance your daily joy by aligning your energy, thoughts, and responses with your highest potential.

"Jennifer is one of the most intuitive and brilliant healers I have ever had the privilege to work with. Her approach, both scientific and divine, cultivates deep insight into who we are, and how we can get the most out of our lives." — Gwyneth Paltrow

ISBN: 978-1-922573-68-1
64 cards and 168-page guidebook set

Also available from Blue Angel Publishing®

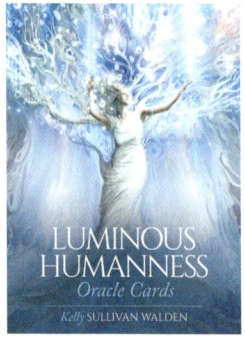

LUMINOUS HUMANNESS ORACLE CARDS

KELLY SULLIVAN WALDEN
Artwork by LAILA SAVOLAINEN

To be luminous is to be at ease with your inner gold. In feeling and freeing your authentic, connected, and whole self, your light illuminates your path and possibilities so you can move forward in confidence and clarity, excited for all that awaits you.

Bestselling author Kelly Sullivan Walden rolls insight, imagination, and joy into this gorgeous oracle, elevating perspective and turning everyday tedium into treasured moments and glowing experiences. Laila Savolainen's artworks allow you to hold the transcendent in your hands and its truths in your heart. Play with these cards for a few minutes each day to invite a more radiant life to meet you, wherever you are at.

ISBN: 978-1-922573-69-8
44 cards and 116-page guidebook set

Also available from Blue Angel Publishing®

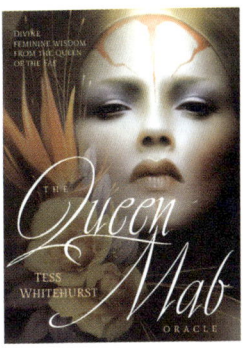

THE QUEEN MAB ORACLE
Divine Feminine Wisdom from the Queen of the Fae

TESS WHITEHURST
Artwork by MÉLANIE DELON & CECILIA G.F.

From all such stuff that dreams are made of ... even now, answers are on the way to you. On the wings of an endless midsummer's night, something blessed this way comes, powered by the earth, the wind and the divine radiance of the Faery Queen.

Ancient and powerful, Queen Mab is an elemental emissary of charm, moonlight and manifestation. Turn to her for meaning, revelation and insight into the poetry and empowerment at play within all that is and all you shall become.

ISBN: 978-1-922573-77-3
45 cards and 160-page guidebook set

Also available from Blue Angel Publishing®

Practical Magic
An Oracle for Everyday Enchantment

Serene Conneeley
Artwork by Selina Fenech

Energise the purpose, knowledge, and potential within you to empower your heart and transform your tomorrows. This inspired collaboration is a rich compendium of fascination, insight, ritual, symbolism, and divination that you can action in your daily life for surprising and satisfying results.

Journey into initiation and possibility, welcome adventure and reward, set nurturing boundaries, and shape your reality with the support of deities, herbs, crystals, colour, the elements, and intention. Believe in your innate powers of creation and innovation, and charge your world with wonder — now and always.

ISBN: 978-1-922573-70-4
36 cards and 304-page guidebook set + card stand

Also available from Blue Angel Publishing®

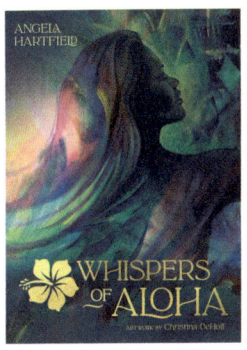

Whispers of Aloha

Angela Hartfield
Artwork by Christina DeHoff

Embrace the bliss, empowerment, and spirit of Aloha through Angela Hartfield's oracular ode to her island home. In her signature style, Angela illuminates the wisdom within the artworks, so they convey personal meaning for detailed and revelatory readings. The lush imagery by Maui-based Christina DeHoff provides a visual connection to the elements, deities, nature, and joys of Hawaii. Revel in glorious inner and outer landscapes, dance where worlds meet, and immerse yourself in wonder as you discover direction, guidance, purpose, and harmony.

With a Foreword by Alana Fairchild.

ISBN: 978-1-922573-46-9
44 cards and 160-page guidebook set

NOTES

NOTES

NOTES

NOTES

NOTES